Connie Albers wisely recognizes that it's relationships, not gimmicks or rules, that form the best bridge between you and your teenager. This book hands you what you most need: hopeful, practical ideas you can use this week to have the relationship with your child you've always wanted.

> **KARA POWELL, PhD,** executive director of the Fuller Youth Institute and coauthor of *Growing Young*

Parenting is hard. Parenting teens in this culture can be downright overwhelming. I'm grateful for wise guides like Connie Albers. *Parenting beyond the Rules* has a terrific mix of stories, down-to-earth practical advice, and tools for self-evaluation, all given without losing what's ultimately important.

> **JOHN STONESTREET,** president of the Colson Center and coauthor of *A Practical Guide to Culture*

In a world where parents struggle to prioritize their families over many pressures, Connie Albers is a breath of fresh air. *Parenting beyond the Rules* is a must-read for every parent who desires a lifelong relationship with their child. Having raised her own five children to adulthood, Connie offers parents more than just anecdotal encouragement; she equips them to understand and engage with their teens every step of the way. The teen years can be some of the best years of parenting. Connie will show you how to get the most out of them.

> **HEIDI ST. JOHN,** mother of seven, author of *Becoming MomStrong*, speaker, and founder of MomStrong International

As the father of four and an educator, I admire anyone who focuses time and energy on making life better for teens and their parents. Connie Albers has taken on the ever-challenging topic of parenting teens with experience, grace, and wisdom. Connie deeply understands that parenting moves from authority to influence, rooted in a relationship that must be intentionally nurtured. This volume is a wonderful contribution and is a must-read for any parent who wants more!

> PAUL J. MAURER, PhD, president of Montreat College

Parenting beyond the Rules will inspire, encourage, and strengthen you. Connie beautifully illustrates her truths with relevant illustrations and stories. They make the book easy to read and help you understand why teens behave the way they do—and how to best respond. Her ideas will help you stay connected to your teens as you prepare to launch them into the next phase of their lives. That's a definite strength of this book. For example, her practical ideas about being aware and available so your teens will engage with you are excellent. Read this now!

> KATHY KOCH, PhD, founder of Celebrate Kids and author of *Start with the Heart*

A needlepoint hung in our home during our children's teenage years, reminding us that there are two gifts we should give our children: roots and wings. We want our children to know where home is and to always feel safe and comfortable there. But we also want them to know how to fly away and to exercise what they've learned. *Parenting beyond the Rules* provides the principles for developing both roots and wings with grace and confidence. Connie Albers shares solid principles for raising healthy adults who will also rise up and call their parents blessed.

> DAN MILLER, *New York Times* bestselling author of *48 Days to the Work You Love*

I can't think of a better person to glean wisdom and practical advice from than Connie Albers. Her vulnerable stories from raising teenagers will encourage and inspire, showing you that you're not alone in the day-to-day struggles. Her wise words will give you hope, fill your heart with joy, and help you improve your relationship with your teen. I will reread this guide year after year as I walk through the teenage years with my four boys. *Parenting beyond the Rules* is a must-have for all parents of teens!

ERIN CHASE, author of *The $5 Dinner Mom Cookbook*

With vulnerability and sensitivity, Connie addresses the tough issues that parents and teens face together, with a focus on maintaining a loving and lasting relationship. Unlike many books that are limited to feelings and theory, *Parenting beyond the Rules* provides practical advice you can use every day.

SAM BLACK, a vice president at Covenant Eyes

Connie reminds us that the teen years aren't something to simply be gotten through but rather an opportunity to deepen our relationships with our kids, even as we prepare for them to leave us. During what can be an isolating season of parenting, we need practical advice and comforting encouragement, and I found both generously offered in this book. I would love a pocket-size version to carry with me into every interaction with my teenagers!

VANESSA HUNT, coauthor of *Life in Season: Celebrate the Moments That Fill Your Heart and Home*

A voice of gentle authority and experience, Connie gives us the necessary, practical, and biblical brushstrokes for parents who have—or will have—teens in the home. She shows that the beautiful journey of parenting teens is in the everyday stuff, not just in the finished masterpiece once they are grown. Connie leads parents in understanding that our job is not just about a set of rules to follow but more about how to find assurance and delight in these few years left with the teens in our lives. I recommend this book to anyone struggling, anxious, or curious about how to navigate the teen years.

KRISTIN FUNSTON, author of *More for Mom*

Parenting beyond the Rules provides straightforward strategies for connecting to the heart of your child. Find encouragement to parent with intention and wisdom as you foster a lifelong relationship with your teen.

KATIE M. REID, MA, secondary education, mother to five and author of *Made like Martha*

My wife and I have spent significant time with Connie's adult children. They've shared stories and thought processes of some meaningful decisions they've made. One thing was clear: They had been parented for more than adhering to the rules—they had been parented to act independently yet interdependently, to think creatively yet cooperatively, and to live boldly yet humbly. We are hoping some of it rubs off on our seven children and are grateful for the Alberses.

JASON C. DUKES, pastor and author of *Live Sent* and *Inviting Along*

Connie has packed a lifetime of wisdom and experience into *Parenting beyond the Rules*. Every parent will find golden nuggets of actionable intel from the front lines of parenting. Don't just read it . . . USE IT!

RICK GREEN, founder of Patriot Academy

Parenting during the teen years can be incredibly isolating; we navigate challenges while honoring our teenagers' desire for privacy. You can't ask just anyone for advice anymore! Connie Albers has stepped into the gap. Her combination of wisdom and practical advice was exactly what I needed to read, and I found myself sighing in relief. Connie has been where I am, she understands what I'm going through, and she offers guidance that makes sense.

DANA K. WHITE, author of *Decluttering at the Speed of Life*

Parenting beyond the Rules was a breath of fresh air to my soul. Connie's approach to relationships with her children, connecting on a level beyond rules, was precisely the inspiration that I needed. With Connie's heartfelt wisdom, I feel like I have a mentor that I can reference again and again as we walk through the teenage years with each of our children. Every parent should read *Parenting beyond the Rules* to learn how to form intentional relationships with their children that will continue into adulthood.

KASEY TRENUM, blogger, author, social-media influencer, and momma of four; www.kaseytrenum.com

As a parent of three teenagers, I am beyond grateful for Connie's encouragement. In *Parenting beyond the Rules*, I gained a new perspective of how to guide my children through their teen years. Connie places a strong emphasis on relationships over rules, always focusing on the heart of the child. I am inspired and encouraged that our best years are yet to come!

MORGAN TYREE, professional organizer and writer

Transparent, insightful, and practical. *Parenting beyond the Rules* gives parents sound advice, solid principles, and heart-relevant stories to encourage you in the journey of shaping a teen's life. Richer relationships can be ours when we apply what Connie lays out in this book. If you have a teen or know one, this book has your name on it. And their heart will have your name on it as a result.

BLYTHE DANIEL, literary agent and coauthor of *Mended*

Parenting beyond the Rules provides practical tools for demonstrating love to your teens while communicating and managing your own expectations. This easy-to-read book also helps you empower your family to approach life from a team perspective that will equip your teens for lifelong success as they move toward adulthood.

   MICHELLE NIETERT, MA, licensed professional counselor supervisor

Connie Albers reminds us that we were once teens longing to have wings to travel our own journey. Helping a teen grow into responsible adulthood requires letting go while retaining their heart and their respect. *Parenting beyond the Rules* gives a concise guide of how to do just that.

   JOANNE MILLER, author of *Creating a Haven of Peace*

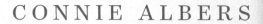

CONNIE ALBERS

PARENTING

BEYOND

THE RULES

Raising teens with
confidence *and* joy

NavPress

A NavPress resource published in alliance
with Tyndale House Publishers, Inc.

NavPress is the publishing ministry of The Navigators, an international Christian organization and leader in personal spiritual development. NavPress is committed to helping people grow spiritually and enjoy lives of meaning and hope through personal and group resources that are biblically rooted, culturally relevant, and highly practical.

For more information, visit www.NavPress.com.

Parenting beyond the Rules: Raising Teens with Confidence and Joy

Copyright © 2019 by Connie Albers. All rights reserved.

A NavPress resource published in alliance with Tyndale House Publishers, Inc.

NAVPRESS is a registered trademark of NavPress, The Navigators, Colorado Springs, CO. The NAVPRESS logo is a trademark of NavPress, The Navigators. *TYNDALE* is a registered trademark of Tyndale House Publishers, Inc. Absence of ® in connection with marks of NavPress or other parties does not indicate an absence of registration of those marks.

The Team:
Don Pape, Publisher
Caitlyn Carlson, Acquisitions Editor
Elizabeth Schroll, Copy Editor
Julie Chen, Designer

Cover art and photograph by Julie Chen. Copyright © Tyndale House Publishers, Inc. All rights reserved.

Published in association with The Blythe Daniel Agency, Inc., P.O. Box 64197, Colorado Springs, CO 80962

Some of the anecdotal illustrations in this book are true to life and are included with the permission of the persons involved. All other illustrations are composites of real situations, and any resemblance to people living or dead is purely coincidental.

For information about special discounts for bulk purchases, please contact Tyndale House Publishers at csresponse@tyndale.com, or call 1-800-323-9400.

Cataloging-in-Publication Data is available.

ISBN 978-1-63146-885-8

Printed in the United States of America

25	24	23	22	21	20	19
7	6	5	4	3	2	1

*To all the parents who desire to build
a closer relationship with their teenagers.*

*To my mom, Fran Lambert:
Thank you for choosing me.
I've been blessed by your love and support every day.
You have set an example of how to be a
generous grandmother by your gift of availability.*

*Tom Albers:
Thank you for being a faithful husband and father.
Your leadership in our home keeps us striving to be more like Jesus.
I love the man you are and the life we've built.*

*To Paul, Jeannie, Tyler, Jaclyn, and Jonathan:
You are the inspiration for this book.
Together, we have created lifelong memories.
You have taught me that being your mom is my life's greatest work.
For that, I am deeply grateful. I love you all deeply.*

*Shana, Amanda, and Josh:
We are grateful God brought you into the family.
You are an answer to my prayers.
We love doing life together and look forward to
many years of creating memorable moments.*

*And to the one who directs our path,
the one who loves us beyond the rules:
Thank you, Lord, for the gift of children and the
opportunity to help build stronger families for your glory.*

CONTENTS

FOREWORD

My wife and I entered the raising-teens phase of our parenting in 1988, when our oldest daughter turned thirteen. For the next twenty-nine years, we had a steady supply of teenage children. We have ten children. Do the math: At one point, we had six teens in our house.

When my wife and I were first married, we had the real pleasure of serving as the leaders of a large group of junior-high kids in our church in Bellingham, Washington. We were qualified—or so we thought. After all, we had been teenagers ourselves only a year or two earlier.

Any thought that we knew all the tricks of guiding teens quickly dissipated as we began to see the complexities of this season of life. And when we became parents of teens almost two decades later, we remembered enough from those youth-group years to realize that we were entering a season that required wisdom beyond our own if we were going to succeed.

Connie Albers, a mom of five grown children, has created an excellent compilation of the kind of wisdom that she gained the hard way—successfully raising five children through the teen years to adulthood. Her dependence on God and his Word ensures that her wisdom is infused with eternal wisdom from above.

Let me warn you. If you are looking for a book with can't-miss formulas and easy tricks to turn raising teens into a season of unending joy, this isn't it. But I'll tell you a secret. Such books aren't worth the money you pay for them, nor the time it takes to read them.

Connie's book will give you some practical suggestions in each of the thoughtfully organized chapters. But don't underline these suggestions and miss the larger and far more important truth that she presents with winsome relentlessness.

Successful parenting of a teenager must be focused on building a great relationship with your child. Connie gives important suggestions on how to do this. But her bigger message has two important truths embedded in these suggestions and her many encouraging stories.

- If you want a great relationship with your teen, work on winning their heart.

- While what you *do* will impact that effort, the most important thing you can do to win your child's heart is to make sure that your own heart is right with God and right with your child.

Connie's narrative creates the opportunity for you to examine your own attitudes and heart condition as you parent. Don't miss this opportunity.

Win your teen's heart by making sure that God has your heart. That's a truth worth knowing.

Michael Farris
CEO and general counsel for
Alliance Defending Freedom

INTRODUCTION

THE PICTURE EMERGED as we were standing in the Panera parking lot, my oldest daughter and I. I was at the beginning of a new parenting season—the youngest of my five children had recently graduated from high school—and so I had embarked on starting a business. My oldest daughter, a talented photographer and artist, was helping me with the branding.

As we reflected on the next steps in my journey, she started making a small circular motion with her left hand. She said, "Mom, you did some pretty cool things before you had kids."

She was right. Before I had kids, I was a spokesperson and corporate trainer. I worked with celebrities, CEOs, and news anchors. I also did television and radio interviews and made many guest appearances on behalf of the company I worked for. I was even given the "Keys to the City" once by a mayor. (Honestly, I didn't know what the keys were for, but I posed for pictures and politely said thank you.) Everything I did back then was fun and exciting.

My daughter took her right hand and began making another small circle. "And you're doing some amazing things now that we're grown."

But then she started a new circle in the air, a larger one between the two small ones. "But Mom, this—" she stared into my eyes—"this is your life's greatest work! Look at us kids. Look at our family. Look at the family you and Dad built."

And that was the key. Everything I've done or will do pales in comparison to having a close relationship with my family.

With tears streaming down my cheeks, I thought, *This is what Proverbs 31 is all about.* That our children will rise up and call us blessed. The desire of every mother—to hear a child say, "Look at our family." My kids know better than anyone how imperfect I was as a mother. They saw me at my worst. They know who didn't get along with whom. They know when I was at odds with their dad. And still, my daughter said, "Look at us." The lump in my throat made it almost impossible to swallow.

None of this happened because I have all the answers. I believe it happened because many years ago, I listened to God and intentionally applied what I learned. And one thing I learned is this: The teen years are not something to dread. This critical season of our children learning to become adults can be filled with joy and rich relationship by parenting beyond the rules.

I'm inviting you on a dynamic parenting journey. Along the way, you will discover why paying attention to your relationship with your teen—to keeping and prioritizing their heart—can yield the closeness you long for as you navigate this incredible season of parenting. Boundaries and direction are important in raising teens, but only in the context of caring well for their hearts.

Often, we parents are so busy managing life that the small, everyday things in our relationships with our children get overlooked. We find ourselves jumping from one crisis to another. We might have even been told that the small things don't really matter. Because our lives are so full, we accept this statement without really questioning its validity. But as you parent your teen, I urge you not to reject what you can learn from the small things. I know how easy it is to overlook the eye roll, the disrespectful comment, the little white lie, or the forgetting the turn-off-devices-at-bedtime rule—or to simply address the action and not the motive underneath. As tempting as it is to ignore the little things, I urge you to look more closely at why your teen does what he or she does.

An ancient proverb says "out of [the heart] flows the issues of life" (Proverbs 4:23, JUB). The issues your teen is working on will flow out. And most of the time, they will leak out slowly. That's why we must diligently notice the little things and help our teens before the seemingly insignificant problems materialize into bigger problems. This care for their hearts and our relationships is how we can keep the hearts of our teens in a world trying to steal them away.

The teen years go by quickly. But after raising five amazing children into adulthood and working with teens for more than twenty-five years, I have seen and heard quite a bit. I've learned what works, what makes teens pull away, and what draws them closer. We have the opportunity to help guide them toward what God designed them to be. And for those of you who are keenly aware of your mistakes and shortcomings, it's not too late to influence your teen. It's my sincere prayer that through this book, you will learn how to keep the heart of your teen and enjoy building relationships that last well beyond the teen years.

The daughter who stood in the parking lot that day, speaking life into my heart, was once invited to paint a masterpiece for a pediatric charity fund-raiser gala featuring Tim Tebow as the guest speaker. As part of the evening, she was asked to stand in front of all the guests and add additional brushstrokes to the piece. Nothing big. Small strokes here and there where she felt the painting needed a little something.

Hers was the last piece auctioned off that evening. And, much to our delight, it sold for the most money. She had never had a piece sell for that much. I couldn't help but wonder if those additional touches made all the difference. Those seemingly minor strokes on the canvas, which no one could tell were there, mattered.

Your child is a masterpiece in the making. And God gave you the opportunity to add little touches here and there as you navigate this critical season of parenting. There will be times you have to use large brushstrokes with bold colors to lay foundational truths. Sometimes you will need to step back and let the paint dry so you can see what else needs to be added. Other times, you'll want to use smaller brushes of insights and redirection to add accent colors, drawing attention to a specific area of the painting. Every parenting word, action, reaction, and angry outburst adds to the painting.

Parenting beyond the rules means knowing the brushes you have to work with and the colors you want to include but investing the time and valuing your relationship with your child so you can improvise in the midst of intentionality. Rules are important, but you want to be able to dig deeper than that, to see who your child is and prioritize the relationship so that the rules don't rule you. When you parent this way, intentionality and improvisation will work together as you paint a beautiful canvas, one that will be enjoyed for a lifetime. You are creating your family's legacy.

Most parents don't feel fully equipped for such a task. But you are! God has prepared you for this journey. Granted, some days will be more challenging than others. I can guarantee it. However, I promise you this: You are able to overcome whatever setbacks you encounter along the way. You can pull out the colors of forgiveness, grace, humility, and love and ask the one who formed and fashioned your child to help you paint over the areas that need a little something.

Are you ready to pick up your brush?

Chapter 1

WHEN THE DREAM CHANGES

I COLLAPSED INTO BED, utterly exhausted after another long night of trying to reason with my son. I replayed and analyzed every part of the conversation, hoping to determine what I might have said or done wrong or discover what I could do better next time. I felt a stream of tears run down the side of my face and soak my hairline. I longed to enjoy a relationship with Paul. I didn't think that was too much to hope for—so why did every encounter backfire on me? It felt as if all we did lately was clash. We got along fine as long as the conversations were surface level or I didn't expect him to talk to me about how he was doing. But that's not how I wanted our relationship to be.

Not a day went by that I didn't think about what was going on with Paul. What had happened to him? He was my compliant child; he'd made me believe I was a great mother. So where had I gone wrong? I hadn't changed anything, yet my parenting wasn't working anymore. Why wouldn't he listen to me? *God, I don't know what to do.*

I feared that Paul would leave our house and never look back. And honestly, there were some days I wouldn't have minded that one bit. But then the rational side of my brain chimed in. I knew I didn't want that. I wanted a relationship—with fun, laughter, obedience, minimal strife or friction. But how could I accomplish this? *God, please show me what I need to do, where I need to change, how I can do this parenting job better. I know there is no such thing as a perfect parent, but I long to be the parent he needs me to be.*

Tucked deep in my heart lay the vision I'd dreamed of when I first held that precious little bundle of joy. I saw a little boy who enjoyed being with me. I envisioned things like teaching him God's Word, taking long bike rides, going on ice-cream dates, playing kickball in the front yard, taking camping trips, going hiking and sightseeing. And for much of his life, that vision had played out as I'd hoped. I loved spending time with him.

As he grew, I began to hope for more profound things—like having deep, meaningful late-night talks where he would invite me into the sacred space of his inner thoughts, the place where parents learn what is happening in the hearts of their teens. Trust is critical if a parent wants to be welcomed into a teen's inner world. Paul and I needed to have a relationship secure enough for him to share hopes and dreams, fears and anxieties, as well as insecurities—all of which require a willingness to be vulnerable. Such openness can be scary for an adolescent; vulnerability can be emotionally risky. I pictured mapping out his life and experiencing a million beautiful conversations. I was his biggest cheerleader, and he knew it. I believed we wouldn't drift apart, as many other families do. We would remain close, and the teen years would be our best.

Unfortunately, most visions don't play out as we expect them to, especially when it comes to parenting teens. Detours and pitfalls cause us to doubt what we are doing as parents. This season of parenting isn't a straight line. It's full of mystery and wonder; it's a series of unknowns to explore.

BLURRY PICTURES

In the midst of Paul's teen years, the picture I'd envisioned wasn't turning out as planned. Paul was changing, and I was at a loss. I talked to peers. I talked to God. I even talked to myself. (Yes, I'm one of those people. Maybe you also have these two-way conversations with yourself, attempting to solve your problems!)

I started to question everything—because I knew if something didn't change, I was going to lose the relationship I'd worked so hard to build. What I was doing clearly wasn't working. After much prayer, introspection, and conversations with those I trusted, I slowly began to change my approach to having meaningful conversations with my kids. Not accusing them before knowing the facts was the first step toward achieving this goal. Then I tried easing up on the rules, but Paul wanted even more freedom. No matter how much freedom I gave, it seemed as if it wasn't enough.

I cried out to God, *I'm failing at this parenting-teens gig.*

Do you ever feel that way? As if you give and change and lighten up, but it's not enough?

Time to teach this principle: Freedom is granted when freedom is earned.

If you're like me, you have a picture of what the teen years will be like for your family. Most parents do. But as an older mom once told me, "You're raising people—people who have a soul, mind, will, and emotions. They will not always be in sync with what you're trying to teach them. And you will encounter conflict during this season of parenting."

Looking back, I see her wisdom. Her perspective proved to be a game changer for me. I began to look at conflict in an entirely different way. I still didn't like it, but I understood why it happened. My kids were people—not just children who complied with my every request. They asserted their independence. They desired to choose for themselves—their friends, their activities, and their future. This parenting season was critical to their overall emotional and mental health as adults; everything I'd been teaching them moved from mere head knowledge to core convictions—the foundation of who they would become and how they would live their lives.

My oldest daughter, the professional photographer and artist, goes into a photo shoot with an idea of what the finished product will look like. She takes hundreds of photos until she feels she has captured what she envisioned. As I accompany her on photo shoots, I pay close attention to the various angles she shoots from, watching how she constantly adjusts the lighting and noticing how much coaching she has to do along the way. She can't just point and snap. That doesn't work. It takes her hours to prepare before she ever pulls out her camera. She has to think about the location, lighting, model, background, timing, weather, and a host of other things.

Parenting a teenager is similar. We have to patiently try—over and over—to help our children understand the vision God has for them. As parents, we have the privilege of helping them become the people they were made to be so God can use them for the purpose he created them for. And we have to do this delicately, allowing them to gain independence and move away from us—first emotionally, then physically.

No matter your parenting situation, I want to reassure you that the difficult days will not last forever. Believe me, I know how you feel—especially after a bad day, week, month, or year. But God is at work. He uses those days to help you create the masterpiece he designed your child to be. During the process, you will need to do some changing too. Teens change; we adjust. It's the nature of the teen years. And yes, many days, the pictures turn out blurry. Each one, though, gets us closer to the vision God has for our teens' relationship with him and with those they love.

YOUR STORY

We all enter the parenting journey with a legacy our parents passed on to us. For some, it is a rich, godly heritage; for others, it's one we don't desire to repeat. I fall into the latter category.

My childhood experiences are not uncommon, though at the time, I felt utterly alone. We all have our own childhood stories. Perhaps you encountered a difficult situation or tragedy as a teenager. Perhaps you had a fraught relationship with your own parents. For many of us, those memories are still sharp. In some cases, you can remember where you were, what you were doing, and how an event affected you. Such memories are what I call *defining moments*. I have yet to meet a parent who doesn't have a story.

My family's communication issues during the teen years compelled me to parent this season differently. Something in me knew the arguing, lack of respect, and loss of trust weren't God's plan for the family. And I'm a firm believer that if we don't actively do something about it, history repeats itself. The good news is, our past does not have to define our future or that of our children. God's power breaks a generational curse.

When you don't know any different, you can't do things differently. This presented a problem for me. Because I couldn't yet understand the bigger picture, I didn't know how to keep the hearts of my teens. Conversations I had with other moms made me think that they didn't either. We make rules to keep order. We place boundaries for safety. But how do we foster a relationship without compromising order or safety? We adjust as needed.

One of the stories I heard while preparing to write this book came from a mom I'll call Crystal. Crystal had a wonderful upbringing. Her parents were loving, understanding, and supportive. She knew they adored her. *Almost perfect* was how she described her teen years. I thought I'd finally found someone who had a nearly perfect childhood! But in reality, perfection doesn't exist. When I asked about her school and friends, her countenance immediately dropped. Suddenly, she was sixteen years old again. Her vivid memories made me feel as if I were standing right next to her the day her mom entered her room with explosive news.

"Crystal, honey, Dad found a job in Ohio, and we'll be moving in two months."

"What? We're moving?" Crystal's face reflected the pain she felt in her heart. "But what about all my friends? If I go to a different school, I'll have to make new friends."

"I understand that, but we'll *all* be making new friends. That's what you do in a new place." Crystal's mom nodded her head condescendingly.

Crystal flopped back on her bed. "But it'll be my junior year! Everyone already has all of their friends by the time they're juniors."

"Listen, I have too much to do to go into this right now. You're so friendly and likable; you won't have any trouble meeting kids and making new friends."

"But—"

"No 'buts.' We're moving, and that's the end of the discussion." Crystal's mom stood, smoothed her shirt, and left the bedroom.

Fast-forward three months. Crystal took her place alongside other cheerleader hopefuls in the gym of her new high school. Though she recognized a few girls from the first few days of class, she didn't personally know any of them.

She heard someone behind her say, "That new girl is way too tall and skinny."

Another girl chimed in, "Yeah, and her teeth look kind of dingy."

Crystal instinctively put her hand over her mouth.

"She's definitely not pretty enough. We don't have to worry about her being any competition," said the first girl.

Crystal's heart raced, and she felt as though she might faint. Was everyone in the gym looking at her, analyzing her, and judging her as not good enough to be a cheerleader? She choked back tears, but it was too late. Her confidence had fled. Though the remainder of the tryout was a blur, she knew she performed miserably because she was so rattled. She didn't make the team.

The sad reality is that not all teens can counter such criticisms with logic and truth. Unfortunately, such personal attacks on how a person looks become life-shaping beliefs.

"I think I might have been okay if I felt like my mom had just listened to me. I didn't want to move, but when I told her that, she completely shut me down. She didn't realize how hard it was for me to change high schools. She didn't understand how mean girls can be toward one another. I felt like she didn't even try to understand my point of view."

Now, as a mother herself, Crystal sees things a little differently. Her mom wasn't trying to be insensitive; she just forgot what it was like to be a teenage girl. This event made such an impression on Crystal that she vowed to pay greater attention to her teen's fears and concerns. She felt that if her mother had listened and helped her navigate this transition, their relationship wouldn't have suffered as long as it did, and her insecurities about her looks could've been worked through long ago. Instead, Crystal spent years needing to be accepted.

I've heard so many if-only-my-parents-had-understood-me stories. These stories hurt, surprise, and challenge us, but have shaped us in one way or another. As adults, we know life is complicated, but our teens don't. They are just now learning how to handle situations as they come up. And as you know, teen crises come at a rapid rate. Our teenagers are writing the stories they will one day look back on. If you teach your teen to work through these trials as they arise, you'll help them avoid wrongly defining themselves in adulthood.

When I became pregnant, I read every book I could get my hands on. They offered differing opinions on the "right" and "wrong" way to rear children. I kept thinking, *There has to be a guidebook.* This got me thinking about the years I worked for Walt Disney World. When guests arrived at the ticket counter, a cast member handed them a guidebook featuring a map of the park and descriptions of each themed area. It was simple. The problem was, most of the guests didn't read the guidebooks. (If you've done the same thing, no worries; you aren't the only one.) Nonetheless, I was sure there had to be a guidebook for parenting teens.

I reasoned that if Walt Disney created Walt Disney World and helped design the guidebook so guests could have a more enjoyable experience, then surely God, who created humans, had something that outlined his expectations of parents. As it turned out, he did: his Word. So I started reading it. Not as a book, but as a personal letter from a Father instructing parents in how to love and live and parent well. As David wrote in the book of Psalms, "You know me inside and out, you know every bone in my body; you know exactly how I was made, bit by bit, how I was sculpted from nothing into something" (Psalm 139:15, MSG). I knew that if I was that special to God, then my child would be equally special to him. I used this as my starting point. Then, over time, I found other good books by mothers who had survived parenting. I needed to know what pitfalls to avoid, how to maneuver detours, how to guide my kids, and when it was okay to chill out.

Realizing that the Bible could work as my guidebook revolutionized my parenting. I became convinced that families didn't have to live with constant tension, strife, or angry outbursts. If we read and trust God's Word, we have no reason to be confused, angry, hurt, resentful parents. I could let go of painful childhood memories. The generational patterns of my past could be broken. I didn't have to keep trying to find fun in the middle of dys*fun*ction. I gained comfort from knowing that relationships could be cultivated, even during the teen years.

I also realized that cultural norms (yelling, belittling, and disrespecting, to name a few) didn't have to define my family either. But changing those patterns—keeping the hearts of our kids—required surrender. Surrender of self. Surrender of control. Surrender of pride. Once we understand our children need safety, belonging, and identity, then we can humble ourselves enough to change our parenting so our teens can flourish and our families can enjoy doing life together.

Sure, we can put up boundaries, create a bunch of rules, give unfettered freedom, and lecture until we are blue in the face (my kids will say I was a world-class lecturer), but none of those externals deal with what matters most—your teen's heart. The key to their heart comes by way of relationship, not rules. We need to help them figure out who they are and what they are created to be. Yes, there is a place for rules and boundaries. We certainly don't want to throw out the rules! But we don't want the rules to take the place of the relationship. By merely focusing on external behavior, we risk losing the internal war.

Learning to focus on our relationships with our teens requires going beyond a set of rules and connecting on a deeper level. As we do this, we increase our influence in our teens' lives and keep their hearts. And when we develop trust with our teens through the strength of our relationships, we create family cultures in which confidence and joy flourish.

YOUR PARENTING STYLE

Understanding your story and the parenting lessons—positive and negative—that you've learned from your own parents is part of the intentional way you can choose to parent your own teen. Parenting styles are another element of this process. Most of us gravitate toward a particular style of parenting, even if we can't describe what it is. Some of us use any technique that works on any given day!

My parents believed it was their job to lay down the law, and we were to do as we were told. I had no problem with that because at least I knew the boundaries. I felt safe knowing what was required of me. My brother, on the other hand, thought of rules as mere suggestions. If he felt like following directions, he would; and if he didn't, then he accepted the consequences. It was like a game of chess to him. I think he was secretly hoping to say "Checkmate." I know he drove my parents crazy at times. I had a different strategy—the watch-what-he-does game. I seemed to get in less trouble that way. If my brother's actions resulted in punishment, then I chose a different path.

Everything changed after my parents' bitter divorce, however. The safety we once felt was completely shattered. Neither of us knew what to do in the wake of our parents' split. Once again, we reacted differently to our new life. He rebelled; I retreated. Though we were parented in the same way, our responses were very different. He fought and argued over every single thing. I just wanted to stay under the radar.

Just as my brother and I reacted differently to the same form of parenting, so will your child. If you have multiple children, your children are people with hardwiring all their own, which means we can't parent one child the same way we parent another child. Learning to parent uniquely for your unique child makes it easier to keep their heart and create a home where peace can reign.

Have you identified your parenting style? You may be thinking, *Why do I have to examine my parenting style? All I want to do is raise my teen and keep my sanity in the process.* We'll get to that. But this is a good place to start. Understanding specific parenting styles can give us a framework for how to approach each of our teens.

There are five main parenting styles: authoritative, permissive, helicopter, hovering, and lawnmower. As you read through the descriptions, determine which one describes you.

1. The **authoritative** parent "has been identified as the most effective and helpful to a child."[1] *Flexibility* and *fairness* are often used to describe this style of parenting. An authoritative parent tends to listen and encourage communication and avoid rushing to judgment. When discipline is needed, it is typically just and predictable. While high standards are expected, grace and understanding are offered for extenuating circumstances. Teens comply with limits and expectations out of love and respect, not because they fear the consequences. Teens are less likely to rebel, withdraw from the relationship, or sneak around. Authoritative parents teach kids that they can accomplish whatever they set their minds to.

2. The **permissive** parent is best described as easygoing. Their teen might describe this parent as a "pushover." Permissive parents generally issue fewer rules and give more leeway. Peace, harmony, and avoiding conflict are the foci. The permissive parent believes teens should be free to live their lives with minimal parental interference. This hands-off approach allows the teen to do as they wish, when they want, with whomever they want. The parent may believe this approach creates friendship and reduces rebellion; however, the parent's lack of involvement may leave the teen feeling less loved.

3. The **helicopter** parent. This style of parenting is a combination of authoritative and permissive parenting. This parent believes in having family rules but tries to give their teen more freedom. Fear and anxiety often define these parents. Their teen usually texts or calls throughout the day because the parent requires constant updates. A helicopter parent is well-intentioned and deeply loves their teen. Their teen knows Mom or Dad is never far away. Because the parents give more

freedom, their teen doesn't usually feel smothered. These parents attempt to be protective without being overbearing.

4. The **hovering** parent. Shortly after the rise of the helicopter parent came the hovering parent. Hovering parents aren't just nearby; they watch everything. They literally hover, ready to swoop in at the first signs of trouble. They may monitor their teens' phone usage, computer history, and social-media posts. Hovering parents place parental controls on devices to protect their teens from the dangers of the online world. Some teens describe their hovering parents as too involved because these parents don't allow them to go anywhere without being in contact. Parents are more likely to know who their teens talk with online, what apps they download, and what friends they hang out with. Hovering parents are genuinely concerned about the safety and welfare of their teens, and for good reason: They know the times have changed. These parents tend to be Millennials. The rise in popularity of this style is said to be tied to 9/11 and the economic crashes of 2000 and 2008.[2]

5. The **lawnmower** parent. This style of parenting is largely the result of tough economic times, recent terrorist attacks, cyberbullying, and the realization that kids are competing in a global marketplace. The rising cost of living, the need for higher education, lower pay, and lack of benefits all but demand parental intervention. Lawnmower parents tend to distrust those in authority and doubt that others will have their teens' best interest at heart. They try to anticipate and make decisions for their teens to avoid mishaps and make sure their kids are positioned in the best possible way. They are more likely to call the teacher, speak to the coach, or argue on their teens' behalf. They are well-meaning, but they can adopt a mind-set that it is their responsibility to make sure

their teens don't experience failure.[3] As one concerned teacher explained, parents who adhere to this parenting style "go to whatever lengths necessary to prevent their child from having to face adversity, struggle, or failure."[4]

Each parenting style has its strengths and its weaknesses. For instance, a self-driven teen will struggle with a parent who hovers. He will feel you don't trust him to be responsible. A creative child might clash with an authoritative parent—not because she doesn't love or respect her parent, but because she needs more flexibility than what she is given. The distracted child needs more structure to stay on track, so the permissive parent needs to adjust his approach, perhaps providing checklists and deadlines.

Adhering to just one style of parenting doesn't prioritize the relationship or what is best for your teen developmentally. When you focus only on performance and rules, you're less likely to build a home where trust, honesty, love, courtesy, serving, patience, kindness, self-control, and peace are fostered. No matter your parenting style, pursuing the relationship with your teen and caring for their heart is crucial for their long-term growth and health. As you invest in knowing your child and being aware of your natural style of parenting, you can recognize and adjust your parenting practices in a way that strengthens the relationship between you and your teen during these years of change.

KEEPING THE HEART

Once when I spoke to a group of moms at a conference, a mother came up to me to tell me about her fourteen-year-old daughter. She was heartbroken because her daughter no longer desired to spend time with her.

I listened for a while, then asked, "Have you lost her heart?"

She said, "No, I gave it away."

Her reply caught me off guard. I had heard many responses to this question, but not this one. She went on to say that she became so consumed with life and work that she didn't realize her daughter was turning to devices and friends in her absence. Realizing the current situation was largely her doing devastated her.

After our conversation, she left feeling hopeful. She spent some time in prayer and made some adjustments to her schedule, and she and her husband came up with a plan. Thankfully, this wise mom recognized the significance of what was happening between her and her daughter and made a conscious decision to win back her daughter's heart while she still had time.

Why so much attention to keeping your teen's heart? Because from it flow the issues of life. The heart of a teen is a special place to be invited into. Around the teen years, your child becomes much more aware of the changes they are experiencing, and many of these changes may scare them. They crave having someone to talk to. They want to know they can trust you with their deepest fears. They must be certain that you will not mock them, make light of their feelings, or try to fix everything. When you have their heart, you have influence. Even if they don't agree with you, they know you love them and want what's best for them. This provides the security they desperately need to grow and mature into the person God created them to be.

Your intentional attention to keeping your teen's heart may cause you to adjust your approach to parenting as they navigate the twists and turns of life. The strength of your relationship serves as a solid, sturdy foundation to build on and ensures a safe environment for your teen to grow up in.

You might be thinking, *I can never fully know what is going on in the heart of my teen*, and that's true. There is a difference, though, between keeping the heart and needing to change the heart. As much as you may desire for your teen to change, that's not something you can do. Only the Lord can change a heart. But when we have solid relationships with our children, we can share truths about the one who can change hearts, which then becomes the foundation for good life choices.

Keeping the heart of your teen is possible when you focus on building a relationship, which includes learning about, connecting with, and listening to your teen. Your child is trying to grow up, and you are learning how to let go. One of the most critical things you can do during this season is adjust to the changes occurring in your relationship and focus on the heart of the matter, not merely on the behavior displayed on any given day.

If you are reading this book, then you likely desire to build a strong family and cultivate healthy relationships. That's why learning to navigate the teen years is critical. Laying a strong foundation based on principles that govern the decisions you and your teen make is the first step. Learning how to transition as your teen matures will reinforce the foundation you have laid. Once that foundation is solidified, you can comfortably build on it during the transition years, ever so slowly allowing freedom with responsibility.

WRAPPING IT UP

- What is your story? How were you parented? How does that inform your parenting?

- Identify your style of parenting. Think about your child. Is she sensitive, logical, compliant, a thinker? Is he outgoing, active, independent, creative? Take some time to consider your child's needs.

- How would your teen describe your parenting style?

- How would you like your teen to describe their relationship with you? What steps do you need to take to achieve that goal?

- If you think your parenting style is hurting your relationship, what needs to change so you can prioritize keeping the heart of your teen? At times, simple changes—like letting up on the unbending rules or helping your child handle more freedom—result in a stronger bond.

Chapter 2

THE FOUNDATION
OF RELATIONSHIPS

MARK AND TAMI, cofounders of a summer camp and retreat center, have three children (ages eight, eleven, and thirteen). Mark's job involves working with youth during the busy summer months and leading team-building programs for their corporate clients during the off-season. Tami is responsible for managing the budget and the daily schedule, as well as creating age-appropriate games and activities for the campers. Their children are accustomed to living on the ranch. Life, for the most part, runs smoothly. Every night, when the daily activities of the ranch calm down, they enjoy spending time together on the front porch. The conversation usually entails the events of the day and making a list of what needs attention in the morning.

Something was troubling Tami, though. Their happy ranch life wasn't as happy anymore. Tami started to observe changes in their oldest son, Will. Doing what every caring Christian mother would do, she prayed and then waited to talk with Mark about the subtle changes she noticed. These changes didn't include anything awful, but they definitely deserved discussion. Once the kids were in bed, Tami and Mark discussed her concerns privately.

"Mark, have you noticed any changes in Will's attitude lately? He seems more sensitive and moody."

"No, he's just being a teenager."

"Just being a teenager? Does being a teenager mean you can snap at your siblings, or complain about everything, or not help around the house? I've heard him name-calling and belittling the other kids. The other day, Sarah came into the kitchen crying because Will told her she isn't as smart as he is."

Mark quietly listened, then added to the conversation, "Now that you mention it, Will has been acting disrespectfully when I ask him a question. Any question. Even simple how-are-you-doing questions."

They sat in silence for a while, thinking more about Will's behavior.

Staring at Will's bike lying in the grass, Mark continued, "I've been letting things slide, attributing it to having a bad day. I guess I was hoping it was just a phase he'd outgrow."

"But if we don't do something now, I fear it will only get worse," Tami insisted.

The more they talked, the more they realized they were entering uncharted territory. Tami admitted she was dreading the teen years. She thought their good parenting skills coupled with having a close family would let them sail through these years with only minor ripples. Isn't that what we all desire?

As the months passed, the talking back increased. Only now they were being ignored and lied to frequently. And forget about helping—all Will wanted to do was hang out in his bedroom, playing video games and checking on friends through social media. Mark and Tami became more and more frustrated. The tension was mounting. They knew they could not ignore his behavior any longer.

Will was, like most teens, trying to grow up. The natural desire to spread their wings and seek independence often causes a teen to act in ways that many parents find unacceptable. Now, I am not saying that Will's actions were right, but what if you choose to look at your child's outward behavior through a different lens? Through the lens of a teen. Your patience and perspective will change.

Mark's background in counseling gave him insights on building relationships that he used with Will. Year after year, he observed the same basic need from the campers and retreat attendees: the desire for relationships with others. Some arrived eager to meet new people; others were a bit more hesitant. By the end, if the ranch staff did their job well, everyone left with at least a handful of new friends.

Mark mentioned to Tami something he had noticed: The hardest group to work with was the teenagers. They seemed to require extra time and attention.

Parents forget that teens need a little extra time and attention. Too often, we rely on our successful parenting during the younger years to carry us through the teen years. While our parenting laid a strong foundation when the children were younger, that work doesn't end when we reach the teen years. The message many parents hear (and some believe) is to step aside and let teens figure out life on their own. Or, like Mark, they think that it's just a phase they'll outgrow. But the opposite is true. Good parenting doesn't always equal easy parenting during the teen years.

In every season of parenting, we need to be aware of what our kids are going through. We don't stop with the foundation; we build on it. We keep building character. We keep building the relationship. We keep building trust.

I once thought as Mark and Tami did. If I were consistent in teaching each child, if I focused on being available when they needed me, if I approached all that we did in a team-like manner, then the teen years would be blissful. So when one of our children started to pull away emotionally, I began questioning myself. *Was it me or their dad? Did we miss something? Was there a book I failed to read?* It is normal to question what you, the parent, are doing or have done. There is wisdom in self-examination. You learn healthy ways to improve your parenting style without tearing yourself down.

One truth I've learned is that at the base of any strong structure is a solid foundation—a foundation designed with the soil in mind.

My father-in-law taught me about the importance of soil. One afternoon, my husband and I stopped by my father-in-law's office for a short visit. While we waited for his meeting to finish, I walked around the lobby, looking at the designs he proudly displayed. The wall space wasn't large enough to showcase fifty years of unique architectural designs.

When he walked out to greet us, I had to ask, "What's the first thing you consider before starting a new design project?"

"The soil," he said quickly. We talked about the importance of having good soil. If the soil is too soft, the building could shift. If it is too wet, the building will sink.

"What happens if the soil is too rocky—what then?" I asked.

He said, "If the soil is too rocky, the ground has to be tilled until the soil is at a point where a structure can be built in that location."

His words reminded me of the wise woman in Proverbs 31:16. She looks over a field and buys it. She knows what my father-in-law knows: The foundation matters. The soil may differ from region to region, requiring specific knowledge of the area where the structure is to be built. The builder also needs to consider the unique design options available and how to prepare the soil. And so it goes for parenting teens. The essentials for building a strong relational foundation are love, trust, honesty, teamwork, and openness. In fact, regardless of age, background, or ethnicity, these things are crucial to every healthy relationship, not just during the teen years.

RELATIONSHIP, RELATIONSHIP, RELATIONSHIP

In the beginning, I had hopes of raising the perfect family. If we had a good plan and followed it to the letter, all would be good. Or so I thought. It didn't take long for me to realize that there isn't a formula or secret code to raising perfect, problem-free children. So what is the key to teaching our teens to move beyond a set of rules?

Years ago, a friend gave me the book *The Relational Soul*. I thanked her, put the book on a stack of other books I've been given, and forgot about it. I wasn't sure why she thought I needed to read about soul care. Then, a couple of years later, my relationship with my daughter became strained. I sorted through my pile of books and read the back cover: "At the core of our being is this truth—*we are designed* for *and defined* by *our relationships*."[1] I was hooked. According to Richard Plass and James Cofield, "We were born with a relentless longing to participate in the lives of others. . . . We cannot *not* be relational."[2] Plass and Cofield explained that we could not exist well without connection and communion with one another: "Relational reactivity and alienation is death for the soul."[3] I was reminded of my daughter's need for connection.

Think back to the moment you first held your baby. The relational bond began to form. The unconditional, unearned, unexpected love and joy you experienced were indescribable. That infant personified perfection and beauty. And your baby did nothing but belong to you!

Your baby didn't have to meet any expectation to get your love. The 24-7 demands on your schedule didn't change your feelings one bit. As your child began rolling over, crawling, standing, and walking, her actions were met with enthusiasm and encouragement. Unconditional love was not something you had to muster up; it freely flowed.

As we entered the teen years, I began to see subtle changes with our firstborn. Little things, like not answering us the way he was taught, not being as quick to help, not finishing schoolwork, or not looking me in the eyes when I talked to him. For a while I, like Mark and Tami, ignored it. We were all busy, and distractions happen. But eventually, it became very clear: What had always worked in parenting would not work during our next season of life—and I was going to need to give Paul that same unconditional love I'd found so easy to give when he was a baby. Not to mention knowledge, understanding, a very large dose of patience . . . and a great deal of time on my knees.

Building a close family will be one of the greatest challenges of your life. But it's so worth it. The teen years shouldn't be something we just try to survive. We want to instead build a solid structure— something that will last as our children become adults—brick by brick. And contrary to what many of us think or have experienced, rules themselves are not the way to get there. Boundaries and rules are important and healthy, but they function best in the context of relationship. Creating this type of healthy relationship with your teen looks like establishing trust, allowing freedom, communicating well, and staying consistent. Teaching teens to apply the principles behind the rules—rather than just enforcing rules—is, in many ways, expressing trust and respect. As we communicate and stay consistent in this approach, our teens learn to live life, not because they fear punishment, but out of respect for authority, others, and themselves.

Establish Trust

Numerous books, workshops, and marriage or leadership conferences focus on how and why to build trust, as well as how to measure trustworthiness. Words like *confidence, assurance, credence, reliability, strength,* and *certainty* are used to define trust. Trust is a fundamental aspect of healthy relationships. Trust helps us have challenging conversations in safe ways, to know that we're loved even amid conflict.

On the other hand, a lack of trust is blamed for broken marriages, employee-client conflicts, and political unrest. Distrust often leads to suspicion, resentment, anger, and hurt. Conflict and brokenness arise when truthfulness is absent.

Trust is crucial for the parent-teen relationship. Trust expert and author Charles Feltman breaks trust down into four assessments we make in deciding to trust someone: We evaluate their sincerity, reliability, competence, and care.[4] *Sincerity* means that you are honest, that you say what you mean and mean what you say, that you can be believed and taken seriously. Teens need to know that words matter. This happens when a person's actions align with their words. *Reliability* simply means keeping promises. In the busyness of life, we can inadvertently make promises without fully thinking them through; hastily made promises are sometimes difficult to keep. *Competence* is knowing whether you have the skills to do what you say you will do. If you don't know how to do something, it's okay to admit that to your teen. Your honesty serves as a conduit to building trust. *Care* is having the other person's best interest in mind. When a teen knows you have their best interest in mind and you communicate that well, they gain a deeper respect for you. In turn, they are more likely to listen to what you are saying. According to Feltman, care is "most important for building lasting trust."[5]

The trust you cultivated with your child when they were younger can erode quickly during the teen years if not diligently guarded. The influence of friends and others, coupled with a perceived distrust from a parent, can wreak havoc in the relationship.

One foundational way to establish trust with your teen is through healthy open communication. It's critical to understand the reasoning behind your teen's actions, and for them to understand the wisdom behind your words. Open communication takes place when you and your teen talk with each other. It usually starts by creating an atmosphere of what I like to call *share without shame*. Teens will talk to a parent whom they feel safe with. They will not risk being open if they sense shame or ridicule.

Once, after speaking at a conference, I decided to sit in on a workshop being given by a young entrepreneur. At the time, he was in his late twenties, recently married, and expecting his first child. He started several companies in his late teen years and designed products after school. During the Q and A, someone asked what his parents did to encourage him to start his own business at such a young age. I was interested in his answer. My older children were fourteen and fifteen years old at the time, and the thought of helping them become young entrepreneurs intrigued me. I felt sure he would share a business strategy for high-school students that would benefit my children. Maybe they would become the next tech genius and gallery artist!

He was quiet for several moments. He looked down, fidgeted with his notes, glanced at his smiling wife, and then slowly made eye contact with the woman who asked the question. After briefly closing his eyes and taking a deep breath, he began sharing his story.

"I was a very difficult teen to raise," he said. "I fought endlessly with my parents, sometimes just because I wanted to see who would win the argument of the day. I wanted freedom; my parents wanted control. Who would emerge the victor? At least, that's what it felt like to me, a young man who was trying to grow up."

Work was his only way of escape from the daily expectations of his parents. He was completely frustrated—they didn't listen or try to understand. They were in a battle, and the lines were clearly drawn. There would be no winners, only losers. Over the years, his frustration turned to resentment and anger. All trust was shattered by the age of eighteen, and with trust gone, so went hope for a loving relationship with his parents.

When the crowd left, I walked up to introduce myself and asked if he would explain something to me. "What did you mean by your statement 'I wanted freedom; my parents wanted control'?"

He looked straight at me. "I wanted to explore, be adventurous, and discover who I was. All I wanted was to become the person I was created to be. My parents took this as rebellion. No matter what I said, if it didn't fit their model of what was right, I was told I was acting rebellious. I started to believe that all they wanted to do was control me. We were locked in a power struggle. Sadly, we developed a great deal of distrust between us. This lack of trust hurt not only our relationship but their relationships with my siblings as well."

"May I ask one more question? What's the current status of your relationship?"

He dropped his head, and my heart sank. When he looked up at me, I saw his red, tear-filled eyes. "We have not been able to work through the hurt, grief, pain, and regrets caused by our words and actions. There is no trust or respect."

His words had a profound impact on me. This young man had been stuck in a never-ending battle with his parents. And all he wanted was to be loved for who he was.

Some would say he was just a rebellious teen who only wanted his way, and his parents did the right thing by not giving in to his bad behavior. Others may think the parents were unbending, too strict, and overbearing. In all honesty, there was a breakdown in communication on both sides. But the parent is the parent, the one with the maturity and understanding to recognize that their child is acting out of immaturity and trying to find their identity. The parent must be the one to pursue trust when the teen is pulling away. At that moment, listening to this young man's story, I made a conscious decision to make myself listen to my teen's point of view, even if I didn't agree with it. And let me tell you, that choice required a lot of wisdom and self-control from me in the years to come!

Each family must be built on the relational principles of mutual respect, trust, consistency, communication, and teamwork. When the relationship is a priority, teens are able to share the why behind their wants, the need behind their desire. The openness in this kind of conversation, and the parent's choosing to honor their teen through listening well, increase the teen's willingness to accept the wisdom of their parent's instruction.

Your teen doesn't want to be told what to do. They don't want to be talked at. They want to have a conversation *with* you. When they hear you explain your decisions based on your own story, they become emotionally involved. Developing this type of relationship takes time. And it starts with the small things.

- **Spend time.** You must spend time with your teen in order to understand each other. I know you have heard many times that parenting takes time. There is no substitute for time—and it is finite. We live in a culture where time is at a premium. When you become intentional about time creation, however, you will see a difference in how everyone works together.

- **Create an environment of grace.** When your teen makes a mistake, a warm emotional thermostat in the home will make it easier for them to show repentance and ask forgiveness. Remembering that you are not always right and your teen is not always wrong goes a long way in fostering trust.

- **Model repentance.** When you make a mistake, the magical words "I'm sorry. Please forgive me" are like a soothing oint-ment to a wound. You are modeling the example of repentance for your child, and they will model it to your grandchildren. You are saying that we all make mistakes, that we all can admit when we are wrong, ask forgiveness, and continue to walk in this relationship without fearing a loss of love or trust. True repentance and forgiveness are a two-way street. Your teen needs to be able to come to you, and you need to go to them when mistakes are made.

Allow Them to Earn Freedom

Teens naturally start to desire more freedom, and freedom to them sometimes means doing things we wouldn't approve of. As the parent, you are expected to teach and guide your teen. Not every desire, want, or experience will be granted. But taking the time to build a trusting relationship means that saying no doesn't have to lead to a battle.

Your teen needs to understand your desire is not control. We parents do have this controlling tendency, partly out of habit and partly out of fear. We fear our precious children will do something foolish and get into trouble. I know. I had to work through it too! Every caring parent gets concerned. While these feelings are valid, you must remember that God has a plan for his children, and you need to show your teen a level of respect and trust as they prove they have the maturity to handle freedom.

Teach your teen to understand that freedom is earned. Freedom isn't granted simply because they reach a certain age. Age is just a number. Freedom comes with maturity. If your child has proved and demonstrated they can be trusted (and if their desire is appropriate for their age), then more freedom is given. If not, then it will be withheld until a later time.

My five children have very different temperaments, and their maturity levels and areas of wanting freedom were not all the same. A blanket rule or guideline based on age would not have helped them grow. Therefore, my husband and I considered each request with that child in mind.

Our kids needed to demonstrate that they could be trusted to go out with their friends, exercise some self-control, and not get into trouble before more freedom was given. This was a principle we set early on. We frequently explained that some opportunities, such as driving privileges, were not to be taken lightly.

For example, we didn't allow all of our teens to get a driver's license simply because they reached the legal driving age. We had to consider whether they were mature enough to handle that much responsibility. Some of the factors we thought through were whether they were able to pay attention, if they knew the rules of the road (not just what was on the test), and if they had a general sense of direction. Additionally, would they be faithful to apply the principles of safe driving we taught them? We didn't want to set them up for mishaps that could be avoided by simply knowing their strengths and weaknesses.

Communicate Expectations

Have you ever been asked to do a job without clearly knowing what is expected of you? I sure have. It's a frustrating position to be in! The same is true when communicating with our children.

One day, I told my son to clean his room. An hour later, I went to check on his progress. When I walked in, I found him sitting on his bed reading. I was shocked when I looked around his room. It didn't look much different from when I saw it the first time. When I questioned him, he looked up and replied, "I'm finished." One of the mistakes we often make as mothers is thinking our children should know what we expect them to do. After all, we've been teaching them how to do things for years!

I made the mistake of expecting him to do the job the way I would do it without telling him specifically what I wanted him to clean up. I reasoned that cleaning a room is pretty self-explanatory. But what if what we ask for isn't clear? What do we do when our expectations and our teens' expectations don't align? Our natural reaction is to blame our children. We need instead to pause to think about what we are communicating before we say something.

Taking a few minutes to clarify can reduce conflicts. Don't expect your child to read between the lines of your communication. One of the mistakes we often make as parents is thinking our children should know what we expect them to do after one explanation. While that works for some, it doesn't work for all.

Some children only need simple instructions: "Clean your room," "vacuum the house," "declutter the car," or "do your homework." However, those same instructions don't work with every child. For some children, "clean your room" is too vague. With my son, I had to list every task associated with cleaning a room: "Pick up clothes; clean your mirror; dust your dressers and baseboards; clean your window and blinds with an *old* cloth; wash your bedsheets and pillowcase and blanket and comforter, dry them, and put them back on your bed . . ." and on it went. He needed this type of list to keep him focused. Of course, not every child requires explicit instructions. Some of my kids did and others didn't. The key to building your relationship is to parent your child according to their needs.

We would also be wise to remember that teen brains tend to forget certain details, especially if the teen isn't that interested in doing what you've asked them to do. With my son, getting the room cleaned couldn't be the only goal. The real goal was to communicate the job in a way he heard and understood so that he could get the work done without having to be nagged. Communicating expectations goes beyond performing household tasks to building a relationship. And at the root of every healthy parent-child relationship is the ability to clearly and lovingly communicate requests in such a way that the child can succeed.

Teens need us to clearly articulate what is expected of them in any given situation—from understanding acceptable behavior toward others to knowing how to manage negative attitudes to learning techniques for handling volatile situations at school. When kids clearly understand our expectations, we avoid disappointments and misunderstandings that lead to a breakdown in the relationship.

When we tell our kids to stop something, we must also tell them what to do. When we ask them to do something, we should be as specific as necessary. (And remember: You will not be making lists and reminding them how to do everything for the rest of their life! It is only for a season.)

Reinforce good behavior choices by praising your kid. No matter what stage of life your child is in, take every opportunity to praise them when they've done something well or have made a sound decision. If they've made a mature decision that's worthy of praise, be sure to let them know what they're doing right. Communicating well when they succeed is just as important as communicating boundaries and expectations.

Stay Consistent

Teens need consistency. Plain and simple! Consistent routines, values, and expectations laid out in a clearly defined manner help parents guide their teens through uncharted territory and into adulthood. You can't be wishy-washy. If you start governing yourself by your feelings, you start running your family by emotions, and you end up in chaos. Your teen needs you to be intentional and pay attention. But that doesn't mean that if something isn't working, you can't adjust. It means you continually assess the situation. You continually evaluate the closeness of your relationship.

Consistency can be tricky because you may be dealing with other things besides your child. You may be stressed about issues at work or in your marriage, about outside influences or your schedule. So an action or behavior from your child that was perfectly fine one day may cause you to speak in anger the next day. Having a clearly defined plan will help you to be consistent. If you do make a mistake and speak in anger about something that was fine a previous time, be quick to say "I'm sorry" and let your child know you're aware of the inconsistency.

Your child is entering a period where they're going to have their own issues too—they're going to have a lot of homework, or problems in school, or they won't make it on a sports team, or they won't be asked to a dance. Those same internal pressures you face, they're starting to encounter. You want to model your goals and principles with consistency so your teen will understand how to handle stresses of everyday life.

Part of staying consistent is managing it all—your family, your job, and all the other responsibilities on your plate—without losing sight of the bigger goal: building your relationship. You'll find that sometimes you'll want to resist the time and effort it takes to do this. Don't listen. Make time to invest in your teen. When you get discouraged, get on your knees and pray. The strength of your future relationship depends on how you parent today.

WRAPPING IT UP

- In what ways can you improve your trustworthiness with your teen?

- What are two ways you can cultivate trust during the teen years?

- Are you clearly communicating your expectations in a positive way?

- How would you rate your consistency?

- What are three practical measures you can take right now to improve your consistency?

Chapter 3

EQUIPPED TO LOVE

WE ALWAYS LOVE OUR CHILDREN. Don't we? Or do we tend to love them a little more when they perform well on the field or onstage, excel in school, or make us look good in front of the in-laws or fellow parents?

Let's be honest. We have certain expectations of our children, even though we might not think so—and we definitely wouldn't want to admit it. But it's not unusual for us to have times when we withhold love, affirmation, or appreciation. While we would like to believe this is one area where we don't stumble, chances are, we have.

The truth is, our teens say and do stupid things. Sometimes we find out years later, and sometimes we don't. My kids are all adults, and I still hear stories of things they did that I never knew about.

Many times over the years, my kids should have made better choices. While they never intentionally tried to embarrass us, they did. Mostly, this occurred as a result of not thinking ideas through first. This is true of every family. In fact, it's quite likely that you know about more of your kid's friends' stupid mistakes than your own kid's stupid mistakes.

Even in the midst of our kids' bad choices and hurt, we must strive to love as Christ loved: "God shows his love for us in that while we were still sinners, Christ died for us" (Romans 5:8). Jesus loved us while we were enemies! I know you could say, "True, but I'm not God," yet God still calls us to be Christlike. So we should love our children, even in those times they might feel like enemies.

I remember a time when my oldest son crushed me with his words, though I'm sure Paul didn't intend to hurt me the way he did. He said, "Mom, you always assume the worst. Why can't you just see the good I did without finding fault? It's like you look for things that are wrong." He couldn't have predicted how his comment would pierce my heart, deeply wounding the part of me that loves him so deeply.

Having unconditional love for your child isn't a superficial "I love you" statement after a fight or a lecture they just received on everything they did wrong. It's *agape* love—a whole kind of love with no strings attached. It is the love that says, "No matter what you do, what you say, or how you act, I still love you." Through this powerful form of love, you're able to influence your child through close relationship—with you, with siblings, with the Lord. While teens may not be mature adults yet, fully capable of understanding their own emotions, they certainly do understand whether they are loved. Part of me wanted to pull away from Paul after his hard words, but I chose not to.

This true love is not conditional, and it is possible to love your teen unconditionally, even when they don't love you. Showing agape love is a decision you make well in advance. If you've struggled to love unconditionally, why not start right now?

HINDRANCES TO LOVE

If unconditional love were easy, everyone would do it. The reality is that it can be very hard to love unconditionally, particularly during the teen years. Being aware of the common hindrances to love can help us be on guard against those barriers that can damage our relationships.

- **Unmet expectations.** Unmet expectations ranks among the highest as a hindrance to unconditional love. This could include not responding to you the way they were taught, not doing household work, not meeting your emotional needs, hurting you, cheating, lying, or getting into trouble. While none of these behaviors is acceptable, they don't warrant loving our teens any less. Our love shouldn't be merit based. If being loved had to be earned, we'd all be in trouble—because we all fall short.

- **Not giving their best at home.** We might also see our teenagers being friendlier and more open to others outside the family. Because we find that kind of behavior offensive, we resent our kids for it. This common occurrence results from little things that they do, some of which they just don't think about and some of which they don't fully understand. Most parents teach their children from a young age to be on their best behavior when they are out with others. Their friends aren't going to put up with grumpiness, selfishness, or rudeness, but they know their parents and their siblings will, at least for a time. Home can, at times, become the dumping ground. Home is a safe place to have a bad day. For parents, it is wise to discern the root cause.

- **Wounds.** Sometimes we don't give our teens love because we are suffering inside; something from our past or present threatens our relationships with our children. As we all know, hurt people end up hurting people. In order to lessen that pain, we have to be completely vulnerable and be willing to get hurt.

- **Rebellion and rejection.** Sometimes a parent feels her teen doesn't deserve unconditional love because of all they've done to the family. It's easier to withhold love and affection from our teens to protect ourselves because, frankly, they can hurt us. Their words can crush us.

   It's difficult to love unconditionally when you face real hurt and rejection. Everything inside us wants to pull back and protect ourselves from the pain that our teenagers can bring on us through their words and actions. So when they roll their eyes, refuse to serve their families, or act in an unkind manner, we sometimes find it difficult to love. However, we absolutely must look for ways to say "I love you," even when they really don't deserve it. We're compelled to persevere because we're called to equip them for the next season of life.

Through harsh words, nonverbal cues, dismissive actions, and emotional outbursts, teenagers scream for unconditional love and respect. And while you may think they haven't done anything worthy of respect, unconditional love is not earned; it's freely given. Consider what you've done and how you've grieved the Lord—and how he loves you even still. God never stops loving us because of what we do and what we don't do. If you want to keep the heart of your teen, then you must give them unconditional love.

HOW TO LOVE

Teens so desperately long to be loved, which is why they gravitate toward other people who accept them just the way they are. It is easier to love others when they're lovely, and it is harder to love those who aren't being lovely. This is the child God has given you to raise for his glory, and through him, you're called to love unconditionally. But perhaps you feel stuck, as if unconditional love is impossible in your relationship with your teen. So how can you develop the discipline of love as you reach out to your teen?

Remember Who You're Modeling

If your heart is for your teen to accept God's unconditional love, you have the extraordinary blessing of helping them see it. Teens understand the love of God through the lens of the love they receive from their parents; because they can't see God, it is very hard for teenagers to grasp God's love outside of a means they can see. The way you model Christlike behavior provides them with a view of who God really is. If you are conditional with your love, then your teen will believe that God must be conditional. If you're unforgiving, they think that God must be unforgiving. As a parent, you've got to realize the long-term effects of what you do when your child is in the teenage years. Your sweetness, your unconditional love, and your willingness to stand by them through the good stuff and the bad gives them a true picture of what a relationship with Christ looks like.

Study and Know Your Child

Part of love in action is studying your child and learning about their love languages and their strengths.[1] You will find that your love for them expands and your patience for their unlovable aspects grows as you understand what makes them unique as an individual and within the family. When preteen struggles began in our family, I resolved to not just go with the flow and let life happen to us. This turning point in my parenting helped with school, sibling issues, even how I communicated with our children. Though we did not become perfect parents, our parenting was more effective because our love was rooted in understanding.

Love Them for Who They Are

Dr. Kathy Koch, founder of Celebrate Kids, reminds parents, "Love the child you have, not the one you wish you had." If we are really honest, we'll admit that it can be hard to love our children for who they are. We want them to be more outgoing or less talkative. We try to make them stop asking so many questions or arguing over who is right. But love means accepting who your teen is at the core—who God made them to be: their natural tendencies, the traits they will most likely carry into adulthood. The child who is soft spoken or loud will generally remain this way as an adult. The child who thinks everything you say is open for debate or who looks for ways to poke holes in your logic can learn self-restraint, but their first impulse will still be to speak up. Or perhaps your child is a self-starter who seems to do just fine without being reminded to get things done.

These aren't necessarily character qualities I'm talking about. We develop character qualities over time. But when we start with the premise that our children are children of God and are loved as much as we are, we can see their innate traits as God-given.

In this critical learning time, our teens are aware of when they're not being lovable; loving them in these moments, just for who they are, is a powerful gift. Of course, love does not mean no consequences for wrong decisions or for causing hurt. But teaching children about unconditional love reminds me of the Bible verse that says, "Perfect love casts out fear" (1 John 4:18). They will experience consequences, but they don't ever have to fear loss of relationship. If you focus on loving your child for who they are—not what they do or how they compare to other teens—your ability to love them will grow.

Show Love in Meaningful Ways

Loving your child needs to be consistent and meaningful. Consistency happens as you show love daily, even in little ways. It can be something as simple as taking your daughter shopping at the mall or getting ice cream with your son. It can be making a favorite dinner or watching a beloved movie together. Love is also meaningful, shown in intentional ways as unique as each of your children. Look for creative ways to say "I love you" that will speak to that individual child's heart.

I often prayed that the ways we tried to show love to our children would matter to them, because there were times I wasn't so sure. Then I saw a picture that Jaclyn posted—the purple roses we gave her for Valentine's Day, next to a dozen dried roses. The caption? "This year and last year . . . I keep 'em all." Then, a couple of years later, I scrolled through Jeannie's social-media account and found a picture of the orange roses we gave her. She shared, "For as long as I can remember, my family has celebrated Valentine's Day. So while much of the single world hates it, I actually love it . . . because love does exist beyond just romance. Thanks for the orange roses, Momma Bear."

Meaningful loving action doesn't have to be a dozen roses. It could be a note tucked in a gym bag or a plate of food in the refrigerator with their name on it or their favorite candy bar left on their pillow. Get creative. Find little things that will mean something to your child and do them. They will recall those acts of love for years to come.

Be Thankful in Love

Teens are going through many things developmentally. Their brains are developing at a rapid rate. They are learning deeper levels of processing, complex reasoning, and logic. At the same time, it may appear that they've never been taught how to clean, how to pick out clothes, or how to serve their families. At times, you may wonder what happened to that sweet child you once had. If that's the phase they're in, keep remembering that you're setting the stage for the future by modeling what they can be like when they are parents. Model for them the grace that God shows you. Be thankful in love.

How can we be thankful in love? It starts with being grateful for what our teenagers do. Catch them doing sweet, thoughtful, and kind things that you expect them to do, and acknowledge those behaviors. Be intentional to recognize their effort. Don't lower your expectations; just remember to continually be thankful.

UNCONDITIONAL

I spoke recently with someone who has had a difficult relationship with in-laws. It's a story some of you might have experienced: If she and her husband did what the parents wanted them to do, then the parents were happy, but if they didn't, then the parents would withhold love and affection, even from their grandchildren. The whole relationship was built on conditional love. This young couple made a decision to be different: They chose to love the parents unconditionally and not expect more of them than they're able to give. Sometimes people just can't give more than they know how to give, whether love was never modeled to them or they use conditional love to control people. We do the same thing with our kids if we love them when they make us look good but come down on them if they make us look bad.

We shouldn't be so focused on ourselves that we don't see what's good for our teens. Supportive, unconditional love really seeks to bless other people without the expectation that you will get something in return. Chances are, it might never come back to you; however, that's not your responsibility. You're not called to manipulate a situation to get what you want out of it; you're called to love, you're called to show grace, and you're called to teach and train. Be faithful about doing that. I don't know many people who strive for approval from a disapproving parent. They may for a while, but eventually, they'll quit. When you are always there cheering on your teen, they will eventually appreciate your actions. Their genuine desire at that point is to please you, not disappoint you. Your child wants you to know how much they love and value you.

At a time when one of my children was really running from the Lord, I wrote letters and emails constantly to say, "I love you. We're here for you." Tears ran down my cheeks as I jotted notes. I felt the depth of the pain and rejection. This went on for many years, and it seemed as if the more Tom and I tried, the further we were pushed away. This trying time hurt the whole family; when one is struggling, all struggle. If you face such a season, you have to be careful not to take out your frustrations on your other children. You have to take that pain and hurt and give it to the Lord. Forgive your child in your heart. Ask God to replace that pain with sincere love.

The beautiful thing is that through the tears, through the pursuing, and through the unconditional love, your child sees that love. They feel it. When the day comes, and God opens their eyes, they're able to say, "Thank you for loving me when I was unlovely. Thank you for not giving up on me. You didn't remove your love, and you didn't cut me off."

WRAPPING IT UP

- Do you find yourself struggling to love your child unconditionally? If so, what does your child do that makes you withhold love?

- Are there specific ways you can choose to love your child unconditionally, even though you don't approve of what has happened?

- In what ways can you communicate your expectations more clearly?

- Have you examined your heart to understand why you might be holding back from loving your child unconditionally?

- Write down the qualities you would like to see developed in your family a year from now, five years from now, and fifteen years from now.

- Are there hindrances that keep you from fully loving your child without condition? If so, address each hindrance and write out steps you feel God wants you to work on so your relationship can grow.

Chapter 4

THE FAMILY TEAM

JACLYN STEALS THE BALL FROM the opposing point guard, dribbles down the court toward her team's basketball hoop, then stops mid-court to look for her teammates. She hears the coach shout, "Pass the ball" and bounce passes to the point guard, who takes it to the hoop and scores two points. The score goes back and forth throughout the game—they're up by four, then down by two. As nervous as I am, I love watching both teams play. In particular, watching the coaches fascinates me. The skill it takes to keep a group of players focused on the end goal is remarkable.

Although I never played sports, I didn't let my lack of athleticism stop me from being involved in my kids' sports activities. I loved supporting the teams and being my kids' number one cheerleader. When the kids were little, I volunteered for their teams. Then in high school, I helped with each of the kids' basketball teams and Jaclyn's soccer team. My involvement gave me a glimpse of how teams learn to work together and what happens when they don't.

On a sports team, there is something unique about how each player interacts with the others. Every player has a different personality, attitude, and skill set. They all come with experiences from playing with other teams—being the star, getting rejected, hearing praise, or being underappreciated. As you watch, you can pick out the encourager, the risk-taker, the showman, the loner, the player looking out for others, the one giving their all, and the one who is having a bad game. Yet despite all these differences, the players learn to function as one body with a singular focus.

Parents are like coaches. We teach, train, guide, and make our kids do hard things. We help our children learn how to work together with different family members, to do things they don't like without complaining, to learn to do a job well, and to serve others. Every time we help our teens learn to work together, we can teach them what coaches do.

Here is some of what we can learn when we're part of a team:

- We learn to **accept** imperfection
  - We learn that we will sometimes have a bad game; that's okay
  - We learn that we will mess up—and to try harder next time
  - We learn that we might not be the star, yet we're still part of the team

- We learn to **trust** teammates
  - We learn to trust our teammates under pressure
  - We learn to rely on our teammates' skills
  - We learn to let go of being in control

- We learn to **communicate**
  - We learn to work with others
  - We learn to be unselfish
  - We learn to voice our needs

- We learn **boundaries**
  - We learn respect for authority, coaches, and referees
  - We learn to follow the rules of the game
  - We learn to show grace when the rules are broken

- We learn the importance of overall **health**
  - We learn the importance of eating well
  - We learn that performance can be improved with proper nutrition
  - We learn the impact of staying up all night before a game

- We learn areas of **strength** and **weakness**
  - We learn about personal limitations
  - We learn how to overcome weakness
  - We learn to be honest with our team

- We learn the value of **consistency**
  - We learn to push when we feel like quitting
  - We learn self-control
  - We learn discipline and the value of practicing

- We learn **life isn't fair**
  - We learn that life, like sports, requires courage, bravery, and transparency
  - We learn that resentment, frustration, and disappointment are part of living
  - We learn that sometimes things will go wrong

As your child enters the teen years, think of your family as a team. Every team has well-defined objectives or goals, and all the players need to understand the goals and rules. So ask yourself, "What are we trying to do in this teenage season?" Understanding your goals will help you have a vision for moving forward. Rules become the guiding principles that govern how you live and how your family navigates this new season of life. Being aware of where you're going helps keep everyone working together. Your team will be most effective if everyone knows who's playing, grasps the objective, understands his or her role, and learns how to communicate with one another.

SETTING YOUR FAMILY GOALS

What are your goals for your family in five, ten, or twenty years? Many families I speak with respond with puzzled looks when I ask that. After a brief pause, parents typically say something along these lines:

- Survive the teen years
- Make sure our kids know we love them
- Raise emotionally healthy kids
- Prepare them for the real world
- Teach them to be responsible
- Get them into college

Teens, however, have very different answers. Most teens I've spoken to don't think their parents have goals for their families. If they do, it's unclear to them what those goals are. But their answers change when I ask in a different way: "What do you think your parents want for you?" They rattle off numerous replies: to get good grades, go to college, pursue their passions, avoid trouble, get married, and so forth.

I find it interesting that few could articulate with clarity what their families really stood for. Less than half mentioned having strong relationships as part of their family goals. The more I spoke with both sides, it became evident that most families lack clarity and intentionality in building relationships. They just assume it will happen. To hope or assume your family will be close is missing an opportunity to ensure your family will be. You need deep levels of trust, vulnerability, and openness to build lasting relationships within your family. Those don't just happen, especially during the teen years.

When there is a serious lack of clarity about what your family stands for and what your values and roles are, teens experience confusion, stress, and frustration. On the other hand, when everyone clearly understands the goals, each member of your family is equipped to thrive.

Setting a goal for what you want your family to be takes intentionality, diligence, and wisdom. Here are some principles to get you started:

- **Go to God together.** Spend time in prayer and in God's Word, seeking his desires for your family. Consider how your family will mirror God's design for the family.

- **Get away.** My friends Mark and Tami went away for the weekend so they could talk about the family they believed God wanted them to become. There's a lot of value in getting away from everyday life to think about your family's big picture.

- **Write it down.** When we put something in writing, it becomes like a road map we refer to when hitting a detour.

When setting goals for your family, you want to focus on your unique family. Don't try to replicate another family. Explain to your kid that you're going to have these awesome, fun, close relationships and make amazing memories. You might think this sounds cliché, but it works. They remember the pictures your words paint.

Tom and I always wanted to make the goals of our family sound appealing, because that is more fun for everyone. When teens think of the fun camping trip you've planned with friends, or the ski trip you're working on, or the New Year's Eve party they can invite friends to, they become engaged in the memory making. Talk about the mission trip they're planning to take this summer, the unexpected adventures they'll enjoy. Share how you can support one another. You become the cheerleader they'll never forget. If you aren't, someone with different motives may come along and fill that need.

Your mission statement should also include your commitment to working through difficulties. There is nothing wrong with focusing on the positive; however, we must realize that not every day will be full of pleasantries. You will have bad days. Your teen will not always be helpful, thoughtful, or wise beyond their years. You might have a teen rudely demand to have her way, or a teen who only wants to play video games. Teens learn through repetition. Articulate to your family that you will always work through hard times and relationships together.

Parents who've planned for difficult times are less likely to lose their tempers when challenges come along. If your child knows they will be loved and listened to in the midst of struggles and stumbles, they will not be caught off guard when the need for correction arises.

SETTING THE RULES OF THE GAME

Have you ever been to a professional sports game? It's quite an event. My son Paul is a season-ticket holder for the Orlando Magic basketball and the Orlando City soccer teams. He loves watching these games. Occasionally, he invites the family to go with him. It's always fun when we go because he gets great seats!

While other people watch the game, I watch the people. That

alone is worth the price of a ticket. During the game, everyday people turn into "coaches," telling the players what they should do. But the players don't listen to the fans. They pay attention to what the coach and their teammates say. The people on the team are the only ones who know how the team should play.

It doesn't matter what team they play for—players have to follow the universal rules of the game. Officials such as umpires and referees are there to enforce the rules. Otherwise, there would be chaos. Rules help everyone know what is expected for a successful game.

Like any sports team, families have to follow certain rules. And working together for the good of the family means knowing the rules in advance, just as officials remind the players of the rules before the game begins. As parents, we must establish the rules before the need for the rules arises. Everyone in the family needs to be aware of the rules and be confident in their reliability. It is hard to be a team when the rules keep changing. Rules are what keep everyone moving together in one direction while still allowing for differences. Respect for the rules is what makes a family operate in unison.

How do we get the whole family to play by the same rules? We need to start with the foundation.

- **Establish the rules.** Which rules are right for your family? One of our family's rules was no grumbling or complaining. When one starts, others quickly join in. So nix that right away. What are your nonnegotiables? Our kids knew we would have them do a job over if it wasn't done well the first time. A few times of making everyone start over quickly stopped that behavior. You don't need to get upset with your teen when they fall short of the rules; you've clearly explained what they are to do, and they can see whether they've done what's expected. "Close enough" doesn't count when you're a teenager unless the family rules were unrealistic to begin with.

- **Know God's desire for the family.** God's desire is for your family to reflect his character. His kindness, thoughtfulness, service, excellence, diligence, and love can be seen in how well you work together. He wants families to represent him well. Teaching your child how to operate as a team prepares them for life as an adult. When a child knows why your rules matter, they are more willing to embrace them.

- **Work for everyone.** While each member has a role to play, learning to operate as a team is the first goal. Teaching these skills requires identifying the expectations for the family, giving specific directions in a variety of ways to ensure each person understands the rules, identifying which child needs extra support or a different approach, allowing for each child to respond in their own ways and at their own pace, offering choices, and adjusting the approach if the child is struggling.

- **Decide your family values and standards.** Most likely you have a pretty good sense of your personal values and standards. It can be a little trickier to define your family values, since there are more people to consider; however, you can define your family values with some reflection and communication. For instance, not every parent cares equally about the same things. I wanted the kids to respond with "Yes, ma'am" or "Yes, sir" when we addressed them. Many of my friends didn't care how their children answered as long as they answered politely. The beauty of building a family is found in the individual way your family operates. Your values and standards will not always mirror those of your friends. And that is okay.

- **Consider maturity level.** Your goal is to teach and train as you go. While everyone understands and engages with the family expectations on some level, they won't all respond in the same way and at the same pace. It's not unusual for a younger child to be more moldable than an older sibling. Factors such as motivation, distraction, and giftedness all affect how a child engages with the team and how you as the parent can help them align with the team.

Rules are important in parenting. The rules don't change, but how you play the game does. Team players have to modify a play or change how a play is implemented. Coaches have to do the same. They make quick decisions: who takes the lead, when to pull someone off the court to rest, how to encourage the team when they are down. Be discerning. It's okay to adjust how your family operates to fit the moment. What works one day won't work on another day. We must set the rules whereby the family functions, but we parent beyond them. Sickness, crisis, stress level, and lack of motivation require modifying our approach. Rules serve as our base, but how we play the game can change. When we set rules, we must allow for adjustments. Not rule breaking, but considering the family dynamics first. It is wise to not let rules ruin the relationship.

PURSUING THE OBJECTIVE TOGETHER

Practically, how do we develop the kind of family culture that creates a team? It's important to get everyone on the same page, but unless we have a plan for doing that, it's not going to happen the way we hope. As we pursue the objectives we set as a family—both in goals and in rules—gathering as a family in intentional and consistent ways is crucial.

Family Meetings

Family meetings are an opportunity for every person in the family to come together and discuss issues that are important to the health and well-being of the family. As with many things in parenting teens, the true value of these meetings is revealed over time.

I remember when I tried to conduct our first family meeting with Paul. It was a disaster. Tom and I weren't pleased with his attitude, so I thought a meeting was in order. In business, when there is a problem, you bring everyone together, discuss the issue, brainstorm solutions, and move on. Done. May I just say, family meetings don't work that way.

Here is what happened.

I wrote down everything that needed to be addressed on a new legal pad, which was my first mistake because my agenda was pages long. In my mind, I was going to tell Paul what he was doing (as if he didn't already know) and how he needed to *fix* every point. I was so excited. One meeting would solve all the problems. (Oh, if only raising children were that easy!)

Because I didn't want to see his eyes roll in front of me, I chose to send him a friendly text message filled with happy emojis to inform him of my plan. It was so grown-up. But texting meant I got to avoid any negative body language.

"Paul, Dad and I want to meet with you this evening." *Smiley emoji, yellow heart.*

"About what?"

"We want to talk about some of the things that have been causing friction between us." *Smiley emoji!*

"For how long?"

"We don't have a time allotment, but make sure you have more than a few minutes." *Two more smiley emojis.*

"What do you want to talk about, Mom?"

"That's why we are meeting. I don't want to text an agenda."

"I think it's only fair that I'm given a heads-up."

As you can tell, we were already off to a bad start. He knew me, and your teen knows you too. He knew this wasn't going to be a happy, fun conversation. His first reaction to my text was to mentally prepare for what was about to happen.

We can add all the emojis we want, but our teens are going to see straight through any sugarcoating. They know how we operate. They live with us. I'm not saying emojis aren't a nice feature to put in a text, but teens are smart enough to sense when our *talk* is going to be about them.

A little later, I texted him again.

"It's time. Meet us down at the boat dock in ten minutes."

No response!

Because Paul always tried to honor us, he showed up on time. He wasn't as enthusiastic as I was, and honestly, neither was his dad. Tom wasn't a fan of how I'd set this up, although he supported me.

When Paul looked at my legal pad, his defense mechanisms went immediately up. His body language completely changed. His shoulders slumped, his eyes shifted to his dad, and his lips were suddenly zipped closed. You'd have thought he was entering a courtroom without any defense counsel.

Wanting to make good use of our time, I began by telling him we would keep this brief. (I know he didn't believe me—he'd seen the notepad.) I told him how much we loved him. How proud we were to be his parents. How wonderful our family was and how he added so much fun and life to our everyday lives. Then I asked his dad to pray.

The more I talked, the further he emotionally retreated.

Writing this makes me cringe. I was trying so hard to say and do everything right. But I did almost everything wrong.

I'd bring up what he was not doing; he retorted with excuses. He argued; I argued back. He got silent; I cried, begged, and tried again.

After well over an hour of my moving from point to point, Tom graciously spoke up. He was watching Paul and knew that the way I was approaching this meeting wasn't working.

When I finally realized what I was doing, I stopped the conversation. Unfortunately, nothing was resolved that afternoon. The main reason we didn't get anywhere was because of how I approached the whole thing. I lost sight of his being a young man who was trying to learn how to handle this season of life. My attitude was to fix him. His reaction was to defend himself. That wasn't a good combination, certainly not for a meeting Tom and I hoped would build closer relationships.

As parents, we want to build a team that works together, not against each other. We can help or hinder this from happening by the way we approach meetings.

Despite handling it the wrong way in that first meeting with Paul, I've learned over the years that family meetings are crucial for making sure we're working together as a family. In order to keep our family together in the midst of teenagers babysitting, work schedules, and life in general, we occasionally held family meetings and made sure everyone was aware of what was on the calendar. This was not always a formal meeting; sometimes we just had a discussion during dinner about the upcoming week.

Keeping up with the demands of a busy family can prove challenging. When approached in a healthy way, meetings and schedules can help you make sure you meet the needs, concerns, and activities of each family member and that no one is left out of the conversation.

Here are some of the guidelines we used when establishing meetings:

- Schedule a meeting in advance. Try to avoid the element of surprise.

- Make sure everyone has the date and time on the calendar.

- Plan the agenda with Mom and Dad's input only.

- Ask the teen if they have something they want to add.

- Make sure your teenager has an idea of what you are going to discuss and how long you expect the meeting to last. Emotionally, this strategy helps everyone know it will not go on and on. Like you, most people don't want to spend a long time in a meeting. That is why a little heads-up can make your time more enjoyable.

- Talk with your spouse first. They will have a different perspective on what needs to be discussed and who should start the conversation off.

- Open with prayer. This sets the tone for your time together.

- Praise others for the things they have been doing well, or tell about something each child has accomplished. Make sure you mention the positive things that have happened. Be careful not to allow the meeting to be a gripe session.

- State the purpose of your meeting, such as job-related matters, household work, sibling issues, curfew guidelines, Internet safety, driving privileges, or friendship struggles.

- Keep yourself on topic. Don't let this time become a free-for-all where everything someone did wrong is brought back up.

- Allow time for each person to ask questions or add insights.

- Keep your list short. There is nothing like seeing a two-page list get pulled out for an hour-long meeting. Keeping the list manageable will give you more time to really talk in-depth.

- Don't dwell on the problems; focus on creating solutions.

- If you see defensive, argumentative attitudes start to arise, calm things down by reminding everyone of your goals as a family.

Reassure each other of your love, and keep your own attitude in check.

- Make a list of what everyone agreed to and how you are going to work together to help each other.

- Close in prayer.

During certain seasons, our family met regularly, especially if we were trying to work through attitudes or family disagreements or needed to just plain talk without interruption.

Family meetings don't have to be at the same place every time unless it works for your family. I enjoyed gathering at the lake near our home. I always brought a couple of notes (not a notepad!). I learned that our teens didn't want to sit for hours and solve every problem. They would much rather be playing or getting a root canal. Notes helped to make sure I didn't get off track with things that weren't on the list.

Not every family meeting is going to go as planned. Be prepared for tough moments. Here are some things to keep in mind when the meeting gets heated:

- Don't expect a resolution or repentance at every meeting. Teens will not always agree with you or agree to do what you tell them to do. Sometimes they need time to process your instructions.

- Stop if tempers start to flare. You can always come back when everyone has settled down.

- Avoid a negative verbal exchange. Arguing a valid point isn't wrong as long as it is done respectfully. Fighting only escalates an issue. It's important to know the difference.

- Pause and ask for clarification when you sense your teen is resisting your instructions. By allowing them to share what they are thinking, you strengthen your relationship.

- Remain calm so you can listen well.

- If they've shared new information that requires further engagement, tell them you and your spouse need to talk privately and you'll continue this conversation later.

- Remember that they are a young adult in the process of growing up. They will react poorly at times. They might get defensive. They might decide it's time to walk out. While these behaviors are not acceptable, teaching them how to express their feelings goes a long way in staving off such responses. Your goal is to help them express their thoughts in a grown-up way without cutting, hurtful words.

The Gift of the Family Table

Our table changed over the years—from a thirty-six-inch square to a sixty-inch round to a one-hundred-and-forty-inch oval with two extensions. But the size of the table didn't matter. The people sitting around it were who I cared about.

You've probably heard about the importance of regular family mealtimes. Family meals don't happen by accident. They are a deliberate act.

Without exception, all of my now-grown children mention our dinnertime as among their favorite childhood memories. Our children were also involved in cooking meals because we wanted meal prep *and* eating to be a family event. Everyone was assigned a task, including Mom and Dad. Someone would make the salad, another would prepare the vegetables, someone would set the table, and so forth. Making this into a family activity created a pleasant and easier mealtime. We ate together, we cleaned together, and we lived together. It wasn't perfect, but now that I have the benefit of hindsight, I know that the time together was well worth the moans we would get.

I believe these memories of cooking and eating together are the sole reason why each of our kids still makes a point of attending or planning family cookouts and gatherings now. Family mealtimes are absolutely critical to having a close family. While family dinners can be at a restaurant, there is something about being with your own family, around your own table, with the cell phones and computers off, that brings everyone closer. There's also something about everyone collectively cleaning the kitchen together. Everybody has a part—it's not Mom shopping by herself, cooking by herself, setting the table by herself, and cleaning it up by herself. That's not how you build a close family. Everyone needs to be involved in serving one another. Everybody's eating, so everyone comes together for every part of dinner—including prep and cleanup.

The time may vary due to sports or other activities. You could have a slow-cooker dinner so when you get home from all your events, dinner is ready and everyone gets to sit around the table. The benefit of consistent mealtimes is worth the added effort. It's a time where you can see body language, developing attitudes, who's fighting, and who's having trouble with a parent. You can't see that if you're busy and everyone eats when they want to.

There were times where I ventured away, thinking it didn't matter anymore, and because it was challenging to cater to everyone's dietary issues, I just quit. But when Mom quits, the family seems to drift apart. As soon as I started preparing food, the kids came running.

Tips for enjoyable mealtime memories:

- Assign everyone a job. Sometimes teens get distracted and forget to help out. Having roles to fill keeps them engaging with one another. But make sure the job fits their age and maturity level.

- Don't come with a list of parenting issues you want to discuss.

- Listen as they talk about their day.

- Don't allow siblings to mock or put down each other if someone is struggling with an issue. Kids need to know home is a safe haven where opinions will not be marginalized and feelings matter.

- Use this time to build each other up.

- Don't get into fights over table manners or lack thereof. Ask your children to sit up, hold their forks properly, chew with their mouths closed, etc. But stay focused on the end goal. Focus on the relationship. They will learn and apply manners as they get older. And if they don't do everything you've taught them, they will be fine.

- Ask leading questions to get the conversation going.

- Require all hands on deck during cleanup. And if a towel fight breaks out, try to have fun and run fast!

NUTS AND BOLTS

While casting the vision for your family and pursuing that together is a great objective, it can't just stay at the theoretical level. A family culture is created over time by cultivating habits, learning values, managing expectations, and teaching a work ethic. Too often, parents are shamed for making their kids work around the house. This has always puzzled me. How are kids supposed to learn to work if they aren't taught in the home? Society expects kids to know how to work independently, work with others, and anticipate the needs of others. Where are they acquiring such knowledge? I believe it starts at home.

And working together in practical, tangible ways cements the family vision daily.

Learning to work together won't happen by accident, however. Establishing and creating a work ethic requires intentionality, planning, commitment, and trial and error. But the results of such efforts can be the beautiful gift of memories shared together.

At first, my idea of doing work together was unrealistic. I pictured the children joyfully helping each other around the house and doing yard work while we sang and laughed together. It's good to dream, right? You can imagine how disappointed I was when they weren't cooperating the way I expected.

How do we lay the appropriate foundation and implement the principles of working together? The best way is by modeling. Teaching teens to work together takes time. To accomplish this goal, we had to make it appealing, or at least try to make it pleasant. I've learned it's the little things that kids remember: raking leaves or building forts or doing work that draws us closer. Even if it doesn't go exactly as planned.

Establishing Weekly Responsibilities

Getting the house cleaned or the yard work done is easier when everyone works together. With a little preplanning you can pull it off. The good news is the rewards do come later, when your child thanks you for teaching them the value of teamwork.

Jeannie was the first child to move in with roommates. Honestly, I wasn't sure how she would do. Neatness wasn't high on her priority list as a teen. She had pictures to take, music to play, and paintings to create. Now don't get me wrong, she liked having a clean place, but her half of the room wasn't always neat and tidy. I tried everything to get her to help around the house. I made a list and posted it on the refrigerator, texted her daily responsibilities, sent her emails, and gave her verbal reminders, all with minimal success. It wasn't easy, but I remained steadfast, even when I was weary. Why? The goal wasn't getting the work done; I wanted to teach her how to manage a home and life while working with others. It wasn't as if I needed her to do things; I could get the work done faster doing it myself.

She soon changed when she shared a house with four other girls. That's when I discovered she did learn a lot during the teen years. She lamented that no one followed the weekly work chart she created. Or she was frustrated that dirty dishes were piled in the sink every morning. I must admit, part of me wanted to say something. That experience reinforced my belief that our teens listen to us.

Working together cultivates the mind-set of serving one another, which is why establishing weekly responsibilities is so important. Our family regularly talked (during dinnertime or at family meetings) about what needed to get done and then decided who would do which job. After our conversations, I prepared the list and assigned tasks that fit the child's ability.

After I made a list, I put the weekly schedule on the refrigerator and sent a text and an email to each child. (I listed what work their dad and I would be doing as well, because we are part of the family.) When they completed the task, they could check it off. I always saved these printed sheets so I could see which child completed all his tasks, which one did them haphazardly, and which child wasn't doing anything. A simple piece of paper became the proof of what they did or did not do, so I didn't have to rely on my memory, and they couldn't argue that my memory wasn't what it should be. Again, this helps to defuse potential conflict—either the teen didn't check off the work after completing it, or they didn't complete the task. If Tyler asked to hang out with friends or play video games, I'd say, "Well, let's go over and look at the chart." Then I was not the bad mom, and having a physical record of their work helped to lessen potential issues.

Getting teens to clean their rooms or do yard work can, at times, be a struggle—a challenging, real struggle. After years of trial and error, I discovered their resistance was less about actually working and more about doing it in their time frame or in their own way. Once I had time to really think and pray through this, I realized that as long as it was getting done well, I could give my teens some leeway.

This is where principles of serving, excellence, and trust get to be exercised by both parents and teens. Once you've taught them how to correctly perform a job, such as mowing the lawn or doing laundry, you can start giving them some freedom to complete the work in their own time. When you start giving them freedom, it becomes their responsibility to get their work done. If they fail to do it—and they often will!—then a couple of times of not being able to do something else until it is done becomes a great motivator for better planning in the future.

Try to be understanding when teens get older; their schedules can become very demanding. They are up later, working more hours, doing harder schoolwork, and trying to balance their lives as never before. Your understanding and grace go a long way toward building a loving relationship during this season. Think about your overall goal and how much time it will take to reach it. Be patient with them as they learn.

One year, when I was having a difficult time getting my teens to work, I called a local housekeeping service for a quote of how much it would cost to clean the house. I took that figure, divided it up among everyone who lived in the house, and gave each teen an option—either do the work or pay to have the housework done. Surprisingly, they started working again. They didn't want to take their hard-earned money and pay someone else. Now, if you decide to do this, be prepared for them to take you up on it. Don't say or do things that you aren't willing to act on. And don't quit because it is hard. You are preparing them for the future.

If you have several children, one thing to guard against is the older children feeling as though they have the brunt of the work with the little kids not doing as much. In many cases, this would be accurate, but I would remind them that one day they'll be gone and the little kids will be doing all the work. That has proved to be true. There was a time when our older kids did do most of the work, and the little kids didn't do much of anything except being little kids. They did what they could do, and when they got older, they took on more responsibilities. You can avoid resentments by teaching your older kids not to look at what someone else is doing. Remind them they are learning habits they will rely on for a lifetime.

Make Positive Adjustments

Learning to master the art of a pivot is critical to parenting teenagers. And learning how to adjust goes a long way in keeping the heart of your teen. As they grow and mature, we can remain constant while finding creative ways to adjust. We are living, active people. We experience highs and lows, successes and failures. Therefore, we must be willing to change when God leads us in another direction or our children show specific interest in something. Be willing to adjust and resolve issues through conversations as they come up. In doing so, you are showing love and respect to your young adult.

When Jaclyn was in high school, I realized that she had a passion for cooking. So we decided to give her our weekly grocery budget. We gave her permission to create the menu, buy whatever she wanted within the budget, and cook whatever she desired. To outsiders, that was a crazy idea. Trusting her to do her best allowed Jaclyn the opportunity to practice cooking and gain experience. I knew when she lived on her own, money would be tight, leaving little margin for recipe flops. If she tried a new recipe at home and it didn't work out, however, it was all right. We had a full refrigerator and could easily put something together, and then she could continue to experiment with the next meal. She was thrilled with this idea. I had other children who didn't enjoy cooking; they just needed to know Cooking 101 to cook simple meals on their own. Adjusting your teen's responsibilities can be driven by desire and interest as you equip them for life beyond your home.

In this way, you teach children weekly responsibilities they need to do but allow them to focus on and enjoy the areas that give them the most satisfaction, too. When things aren't getting done, talk with them. Ask them why they weren't handling the responsibilities to discover the root problem. May I encourage you to approach this with the mind-set of trying to help your teen? There's a goal here, and that's to prepare them for the next season of their life.

Now, if we had a conversation, the workload was adjusted, and the work still wasn't being done, then we restricted their freedoms. If they didn't contribute to the family, then they didn't get the privileges that came with being a member of the family. This could take a variety of forms. It could mean not getting to play video games, not going out with friends, or losing phone privileges. There would be some loss of freedom—a natural consequence. That is how it works in adulthood.

Use working around the house—establishing, requiring, rewarding for work completed—as teachable moments, moments when we teach our children that if they don't serve others, then they don't receive the blessings of being served. If they don't work well, they won't keep their jobs. When you teach your child to be a hard worker at home, you are also teaching them a principle from God's Word: "Whatever you do, work heartily, as for the Lord and not for men" (Colossians 3:23). Every moment you are with your family is a teaching moment.

LIFE TOGETHER

As you parent your teen, look for opportunities to cultivate the mind-set of doing life together. Give your child gentle reminders that you are a family—a family where everyone is seen and heard. You're all active participants, and you're all going to tackle every part of that—from pursuing family goals to working around the house.

The gift of teamwork manifests itself countless ways, whether it is the ability to work with others as adults, serve others without expectation, or make lasting memories. How you cultivate a mind-set of working together is up to you. You will prioritize the things that are unique to your family. It might be how you establish your family goals, team rules, family meetings, weekly work routines, or which summer projects to tackle. The gift of life together yields rich results.

WRAPPING IT UP

- In what ways can you motivate your teen to be a part of your family team?

- What family rules do you want to establish? Make sure you and your spouse agree. If you don't see eye to eye, decide how you will handle your differences.

- How can you define your family's goals using the sections in this chapter as a starting point?

- What core values has your family adopted? Does your child know what those values are? Discuss and write them down together so your family knows the values, goals, and priorities you want to achieve.

- What conversations would you like to have over dinnertime?

- Define the journey for the next stage of life during your family's next meeting or meal so everyone can get excited about being on that journey together.

Chapter 5

PAINTING POSSIBILITIES

OUR FAMILY LIVES NEAR THE OCEAN. Over the years, we have spent many weekends enjoying the Florida sunshine, playing Frisbee and football along the shore and trying to ride the waves in the ocean. We've made a lot of fun memories there.

From the time the children were young, we told them to stay in front of where we set up for the day. We watched them every second. Once they became teenagers, we allowed them more freedom. If they swam or surfed, we told them to make sure they didn't get carried away playing and drift down the shoreline. Even though we kept an eye on them, sometimes they forgot to pay attention to where they were. One time, while we were building a sand castle with the little ones, the older children forgot to stay in front of us. Sure enough, the current carried them away from our home base. They were completely oblivious to how far they'd drifted, and they had to walk nearly half a mile back up the beach to reach our spot.

This little mishap helped all of us realize the importance of being focused and paying attention.

In the ocean, the currents are so much stronger than we realize. The water swells into waves and breaks, and swimmers get pulled in the direction of the current over and over. So it is in life. Financial challenges, work deadlines, sick parents, bad attitudes, and marital conflicts are just a few of the currents swirling around us, tugging and pulling us away from our goals. Even brief distractions can cause a family to slowly drift off course. Particularly during the teen years, it's easy to lose focus on where you want to go. Juggling your busy lifestyle, different schedules, and extracurricular activities can lead you in multiple directions, slowly taking you off course.

We do not have to constantly be pulled back and forth by the currents of life, although being mindful of the power of the waves is wise. Even though life brings many distractions, we can still choose how we react to those distractions each day. How do we do this? We must choose to focus on the end goal, knowing that the hearts and souls of our teens rely on our intentionality. Nowhere is this more important than in our families.

One of the first things we did when our children were little was paint a picture for the next season of life. We really wanted to set the stage for what was coming next. During our kids' early teen years, we began conversations about the emotional, physical, and hormonal changes they may experience. This gave us the opportunity to show them we understood what they would be facing. In turn, this made them want to share with us when they did experience such feelings or thoughts because they knew we understood this season.

We enjoyed casting a vision for the many aspects of life that lay ahead for our children. Their lives encompass a lot, so we made a priority of talking about their future, friends, family, and faith. We had casual—but purposeful—conversations throughout our day and occasionally during family meals or family meetings.

Casting a vision is not a onetime conversation; it's important to continually have these conversations as we walk through daily life. Talk about and celebrate where your child is living at that point, but also talk about what the next stage of their life will look like.

PAINTING A PICTURE FOR THE FUTURE

By the time your child becomes a teenager, you start to realize that your days with them at home will soon end, and you want to help them to discover who they are and the path God has for them. Get them to think about the future and help them identify their areas of strength and weakness in order to help guide them to the calling on their life.

Discuss different career options with them, and ask, "Can you see yourself doing this?" Challenge them to think about their strengths and weaknesses. Casting a vision reminds me of the time I went fly-fishing. Fly-fishing takes patience. You cast a line, and if a fish bites, you know you might be onto something. If nothing bites, you throw out the line again and again. When it comes to teens, we don't tell them what to do or force them to head in a certain direction. Instead, we introduce them to different ideas and experiences aligning with what we know about their interests.

We did this on a regular basis. Our son Jonathan is an extrovert who works best with other people. He would never be the type of person who'd prefer to work on a project by himself. That inspired us to think about the kinds of vocations that would allow him to work with others. What would allow him to use that strength of being outgoing to provide for his family in the future? To promote an active discussion, we tossed out various ideas—including sales, marketing, and public relations. The seeds we planted led to his pursuit of communications and leadership.

Of course, I have other children who are not extroverts—they wanted to pull away and do what they needed to do by themselves. They did not want to work in the public eye or interact with a lot of people. They preferred to work behind the scenes. By observing specific characteristics, you can make recommendations that align with your child with greater confidence. Your child will not see things as clearly as you do because they're young. Parents have the advantage of a broader perspective on the world and more information about what a specific job may entail.

Use this time to discover more about your teen's interests while guiding them by casting a vision. As a parent, encourage them to explore areas of interest and introduce them to things that they might not be comfortable trying on their own, but do this in a cautious way—their skills and confidence are not yet fully developed. Look for little things they can try without a big commitment, so they can test the waters. Search for internships, part-time summer jobs, apprenticeships. Ask friends if your child can job shadow them. If your teen is nervous, say, "I know it's hard, but you can do this, and I'm here with you. You'll find out if it's a good fit for you or not, and then we can talk about it." This simple action speaks love and reduces the fear by letting your child know you are right there with them—not pushing them, not forcing them, but just saying, "You're not alone. We can do this together."

PAINTING A PICTURE FOR FRIENDSHIPS

Friendships during the teen years can be tough, but by casting a vision for your child's friendships, you can teach them what a real friend looks like. Throughout their life, they're going to meet a lot of people, and some might become lifelong friends. Other friendships may last for only a season. True friends are rare, which is why helping them discern the marks of a genuine friendship is valuable. As you cast a vision of what a friend looks and acts like, you help them manage expectations of future friends.

Girls especially are known for drama in relationships. For example, if a girl's best friend says or texts something bad about her, she's devastated because she is emotionally committed to the relationship. One of the things you should do when casting a vision is talk about what a real friend looks like. Then teach your child not to get upset if the friendship turns out to be only temporary. Your child should still pour into that person, be a friend to them, and enjoy their time together. We don't want our teens to think that everyone will be a best friend. Help them understand they may be friends for a week, a semester, a school year, during high school, or all through life. If you paint that picture in a positive way, even if the friendship doesn't last long, your child can still appreciate the time they spent with their friend. They can continue to focus on the relationship, learn something from that person, and have a positive impact on his or her life.

Propose to help your child discern between good friends and bad friends. As you do this, your child can start to see those qualities and discover whether a friend might or might not be a good influence. Equipping them in this way helps keep them from potentially going down the wrong path. Not every child will be able to readily discern those important character qualities; make it your goal to help improve their ability to identify them.

Consider some of the basic qualities that make for good or bad friendships:

Good friend qualities	Not good friend qualities
Respectful to parents	Disrespectful to parents
Loves God	Spiritual disinterest
Doesn't gossip about friends	Twists the truth
Treats siblings kindly	Easily angered
Apologizes for doing wrong	Needs to be right
Listens to others	Blames others for mistakes
Encourages others to try	Critical of others

PAINTING A PICTURE FOR FUTURE SPOUSES

During the teen years, your child's desire to be liked increases. The conversation of dating will come up as they start talking about a boy they like or a girl they think is cute. Listening for comments and having conversations early on allows you to help them set the standards for and identify qualities of a future spouse. What kind of friend—and eventually spouse—do they want to be? How do they need to act? What will this relationship look like? What are their standards and guiding principles as they enter a relationship with someone? Purposefully get this conversation going. Whatever your approach to dating and teenage relationships, your time investment here could spare them unnecessary hurt later.

Another "pleasant" surprise is hormones. Teens start to be hormonally driven to a certain extent. Girls get a little guy crazy and want attention from boys. Boys get distracted by the cute girl who is friendly toward them. Though our sex-driven culture fuels such thoughts, you don't have to resign yourself to them. The health of your parent-child relationship can be like a steady ship.

God created us with the desire for companionship, including the desire to be romantically loved. These feelings are normal and can teach us a great deal about ourselves and others. So don't make your child feel bad because they are interested in dating. Use this time to help them form standards around the topic of relationships, dating, and marriage.

It seems that the closer the relationship a girl has with her dad, the less she will desire to seek attention from boys because her worth is affirmed by her father. Girls naturally desire to feel loved and noticed. When a dad models how a man should treat women, his daughter learns to expect the same treatment from others.

The same is true with boys—the more the boys know their mom respects them and values them, the less likely they'll be tempted to start a relationship with the first girl who shows them attention. We continually reminded our boys they should not take something from a girl that belongs to her future husband. We encouraged them to get to know girls they were interested in as friends first. And we told them to think about the girl's dad, the one who is charged with protecting her. Learning to think of girls as someone's daughter or future wife helped our sons treat young women with greater respect.

Casting a vision is really about helping your child learn about the plans God has for them, teaching them how to serve other people, and guiding them to be the best person they can be. When it comes to male-female relationships, this perspective puts the focus on being a good friend instead of just trying to get everything they can out of the relationship or have some unmet need fulfilled by someone else.

PAINTING A PICTURE FOR SCHOOL—SOCIAL

To help your teen navigate the social environment at school, intentionally develop the tools of *anticipation* and *preparation*. The social aspects of school can be hard for teens. Their peers can be cruel. Kids witness blatant disrespect toward teachers. Social-media apps are ripe for spreading rumors. Fear of school violence looms in teens' minds. Fights, demoralizing pranks, name-calling, and so much more happen every day, even in the best of schools. It's no wonder kids today experience increased anxiety. They are living in hard times.

According to Amy Ellis Nutt, a *Washington Post* reporter on neuroscience and mental-health topics, "When it comes to treating anxiety in children and teens, Instagram, Twitter and Facebook are the bane of therapists' work."[1] Measuring worth by likes and comments takes a toll on teens' emotional well-being. Their self-esteem rises and falls online if their identities are not rooted in Christ and cemented in their families.

Casting a vision for school involves preparing your teen for the things they will likely encounter socially. By equipping them with proper social skills, you will increase their confidence in handling situations that come their way. Teach them how to avoid the class bully. Explain the value in being a peacemaker and minding your own business. Bullies often look for weakness and insecurity. Remind your child that walking with their shoulders pulled back communicates inner confidence outwardly. Help them learn that being wise starts with discussing how to react and how to behave in various social settings—and let them know it's not unusual to feel anxious or even fearful about new social situations. After all, the chief struggle among teens is fear. Fear of missing out. Fear of being excluded. Fear of being bullied. When we provide our children with practical examples of how they should handle all the peer pressure, our influence increases. Remind them that fear and uncertainty are normal feelings, and vulnerability isn't something we shy away from. Your carefully chosen words give them the support they need to be who God made them to be.

Insecurity defines the typical emotional condition of a child entering middle or high school. Kids want to grow up, but they're uncertain of what to do. If they act like a child, they are told to grow up. If they try to act like an adult, they are told to stop acting like a big shot. They haven't figured out the balance. They wrestle with excitement about being a teen and fear of embarrassing themselves or looking immature. Gently point them to their Creator, the ultimate source for their security.

As your child enters the middle school and high school years, use dinnertime conversations to teach them how to engage in the world of ideas more independently. When they feel prepared with such skills, fear loses its grip. They learn how to become their own person, how to talk about bigger life issues with confidence. With this new season comes the fear that they will not be able to articulate their beliefs intelligently.

Many teens find it exceptionally painful to be laughed at for saying the wrong thing. When they share this type of experience with you, don't minimize it and say they're being silly for letting that affect them. As an adult, you've learned how to deal with such statements; your teen is still learning. The fear of being rejected or ridiculed by peers causes enormous internal stress. If you have been teaching your child your values and beliefs all along, they have a well to draw from. But learning how to implement their knowledge requires time.

Don't lose sight of your goal during this season. You are teaching your teen how to live in the world without being pulled away from the values and truths you've taught them. They will stumble along the way. That is why your presence is important.

Most teens worry about their clothing and hairstyle choices. Even if you've taught them God looks at the heart, they still might spend hours trying to pick out the right outfit to go shopping. Remember the bigger picture—that vantage point helps you enable your teen to overcome other insecurities.

Most teens are terribly insecure about their bodies. They stand in front of the mirror, wondering when they will develop or if they ever will. Boys might do ten push-ups in front of the mirror and look for an improved physique. Girls also look for signs they are developing on schedule. Magazines, movies, and images depict the perfect body type and look, and girls easily compare themselves to what they see or don't see. Because parents can't escape what is portrayed as normal in Western culture, a critical part of your job is teaching your teen to accept their looks and not believe false images of perfection.

Even if you've spent years teaching them that "man looks on the outward appearance, but the LORD looks on the heart" (1 Samuel 16:7), your teen might stumble before figuring it out. Realize they live in a world obsessed with looks. If you're too restrictive, you may invite conflict into your relationship. Showing them grace as they wrestle with this will allow you to speak truth about their worth and identity, helping combat the world's perspective.

Your kid will see and experience a lot when they go about their day, whether they are at school or involved in social activities. Talk about those experiences as a family, and discuss what they should expect. When they tell you about what their friends are doing, be slow to speak. As a family, try not to judge other kids. Pray for them. Your child will know things about other kids that their parents don't know. And your kid's friends will know things about your kid that you don't know. Having a home open to our children's friends gave me insights into others' areas of struggle. It also provided questions I needed to think about in raising our children, such as whether I was truly listening, expecting too much, or hurting them with my comments.

Safeguard your relationship by purposing to not criticize, knowing that your teen may be having a hard time right now. Just love them, and discern the right time to bring up certain issues. For instance, one of the high-school kids we knew was looking at pornography. He was home by himself a lot, and, sadly, it became a stronghold in his life. He talked about it with us one night because we had purposed to be parents that kids would feel comfortable opening up to. We listened, we didn't judge, we offered advice if he asked for it, we prayed for him, and we loved him unconditionally. This young man eventually stopped viewing porn, but it wasn't easy. His experience made us wiser. We became more careful about letting our own kids spend unsupervised time online with friends, and we subtly kept an eye on everybody. We were reminded that you never know what other kids—or even your own kids—are doing when you aren't around.

Teens develop emotionally at different rates. Helping your teen navigate socially requires ongoing interaction and assessment. What may cause them to stumble today may change in a month. Intentionally casting a vision for a healthy social life will help them navigate these changes.

PAINTING A PICTURE FOR SCHOOL—ACADEMICS

When your teen prepares to enter high school, talk to them about expectations. Often, teens think about the freedom and fun they will have with their friends—from playing sports to joining clubs—but fail to consider the academic side of high school. They need to understand that the workload gets harder and that they're expected to be better managers of their time. They need to learn to differentiate between essential and nonessential and to know that the goal is not to just get by but to do everything with excellence. Encourage them to enjoy this season and learn everything they can from their classes. Remind them that every teen is different; they shouldn't compare themselves with others, but they should always strive to do their best.

Make every effort to explain why *what* they do matters. Reinforce the purpose and meaning behind the trials and stumbles they experience. Show support and empathy when they come to you with a problem they can't solve. Understand that they become keenly aware of what they can and cannot do well. Remind them that they are still learning. If they already knew everything, they wouldn't need to continue their education. Letting them know that you expect only their best effort—as opposed to perfect grades, perfect looks, or a perfect athletic performance—provides great relief to a weary teen.

I remember when Jaclyn complained about not being able to do a statistics assignment. Instead of saying she needed help with a specific concept, she said she wasn't good at math. As her mom, I knew that wasn't the truth, but it was a challenge to convince her that statistics was only a small portion of math. I had to think of a similar example from another subject to illustrate my point. I pulled out some of her report cards from years past and showed her her economics and algebra grades. Once I addressed her insecurity of feeling incompetent in math, she was able to work through her mental block and move on to the next concept.

If you didn't struggle in school, be careful not to make your teen feel inferior to you. It's not a competition. If your child feels scorned because you aced chemistry and they can't construct the simplest formula, they won't seek your help. Use your strengths to help them in their weaknesses. When you do, they will learn a lot more than chemistry from you: They will learn love and compassion.

Sometimes teens struggle with subjects not because of a lack of understanding but due to a lack of time management, self-management, and self-control. They have packed each day so full of activities that they don't have time to focus on schoolwork. If this is the case, they will be well served by examining their use of time. Gaining proficiency in these skills equips them for the future.

What should you do if you know your child has been working hard, but they just don't understand a subject or concept?

- Encourage them to keep doing their best.
- Remind them that progress isn't made without being stretched.
- Reiterate the goal of education, which is to increase knowledge.
- Point out subjects they do well in.
- Help them learn how to manage the subjects they wrestle with.
- Tell them not to expect to excel in every subject.
- Be intentional in helping them manage their disappointment and frustration.

Allow the high-school years to be a time for your teen to learn about their strengths. If math is not your child's area of strength, chances are, they won't choose a vocation requiring high levels of mathematics. Since math is vital to everyday life, make sure they have a solid education in this subject, but focus on what they are most interested in doing and where they can experience the highest level of success.

You don't want your child to live with the attitude of just getting through the teen years. These years can be some of their best memories. You want them to become more familiar with their emotions because when they get to high school, they get a little more freedom and a lot more responsibility. As you intentionally cast a vision for their future, they learn principles designed to help them stand strong amid challenge and confusion.

WRAPPING IT UP

- Have you cast an intentional vision for your teen's future? If not, sit down with your teen and begin the conversation this week. It's never too late!

- Does your child know you are their greatest cheerleader? How do you communicate that to them?

- What area is your teen struggling in? How can you start a conversation with them about this area?

- What can you do to help your child understand a positive vision for their present and future?

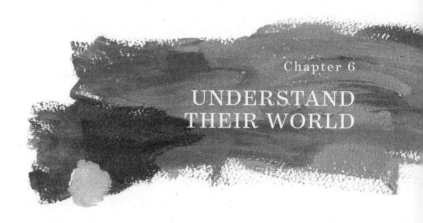

Chapter 6

UNDERSTAND
THEIR WORLD

"Mom, you just don't understand what I have to deal with," my son said, frustrated. I could see the anger in his eyes as he turned away. At first, I thought his words were an excuse to get out of talking.

I responded, "What are you dealing with? I want to help."

"You can't fix this. Just stop trying."

As I sat there waiting, hoping that he would open up, it became obvious that the conversation was over. We sat in silence for what seemed like hours. I looked at him; he looked away. I felt rejected. What didn't I understand?

Does this sound familiar? As I thought about what my son said, I realized I really didn't understand what he meant. Was he saying that I didn't understand him—or that I didn't understand what he dealt with daily? It is true that our teens' world is very different from when we were teenagers.

Thinking about our family vision made me start to seriously

consider his words. Maybe I really didn't understand. Or maybe it was a failure, on my part, to listen. I began doing what I always did when conflict arose: I prayed. I needed wisdom. And so I diligently started to learn what he was facing and how I could equip him to boldly take his place in the world.

WHAT TEENS ARE FACING

The onslaught of technology—the insatiable need for social media, endless video games, and the inescapable smartphones—makes a teenager's life incredibly complicated. It's no wonder parents are more concerned than ever. Trying to understand how to love and guide your teen while keeping your relationship intact takes effort.

Teens are growing up in a world with countless outside influences. Many of these influences are good. But some are unscrupulous. They entice the vulnerable by offering love, identity, and acceptance, which teens crave. Parents who are aware of these tactics provide a level of protection for their children, minimizing the risk through knowing their teens and having a solid relationship throughout the teen years.

As we've discussed, teens need relationships. The desire to connect can become a twenty-four-hour obsession. Fear of missing a chance to engage in a friend's post, tweet, or pin drives them to near addiction levels with their devices. This utter need to be connected affects how they interact at home, with friends, and in public. Once, while we were at a popular theme park, I couldn't help but notice that nearly everyone was staring at their screens. No one was talking to the person next to them; they were talking to someone else. This is the world your teen lives in.

But there is more that parents need to understand. The pressure to conform to social norms, wear the right clothes, and act the right way is high; teens face a world of political correctness, bullying, and tolerance for everything but religious beliefs. If they speak up, they face discrimination, ridicule, and rejection—all of which is emotionally hard and can hurt deeply. Teens are also facing the reality that school is getting harder, and they can often feel anxious or overwhelmed. Taking time to educate yourself on what life for your teen is *really* like—not what you *think* it is like—is well worth it.

Not everything is a struggle. This is also an exciting time for a teen and for you as a parent. You've moved away from diaper changing and potty training into training, guiding, and cheering your child toward their future. They are gaining more freedom: They can choose their electives in high school, they can explore their interests, and they begin to look toward college and careers. And before you know it, they will be ready to launch into the world. Having you beside them, understanding their dreams and goals, encourages them to explore and try new things.

START WITH OBSERVATION

Observation is critical in understanding your teen. You know your child better than anyone else. You know the subtle nuances of their personality. You know their strengths and weaknesses. But amid all that you know, they are changing, and they are facing new challenges. How do they react to peer pressure? What are they insecure about? What makes them feel vulnerable and anxious?

What, then, does it mean to observe? When your child was little, you knew what scared them, what calmed them down, and what made them feel safe because you spent time with them. To *observe* means "to watch carefully especially with attention to details or behavior for the purpose of arriving at a judgment."[1] To properly observe means asking questions, listening, and watching how your teen reacts to the world around them. Keep your eyes and ears open to comments, body language, attitude changes, and friendships. The information obtained is then used to understand. As you understand, you can better share knowledge to equip them for making wise decisions. If you don't take time to observe, you risk not knowing what they are going through. But when you become a student of your teen, you'll discover that your position of influence increases.

When my friends Mark and Tami were in tune with the daily attitudes and behavior of their children, even amid busy schedules, they could teach their son Will how to communicate what he was thinking and feeling. Observation was a wise investment of their time.

Your relationship will grow stronger when your teen sees you striving to understand what they are going through before addressing the situation. You build trust. They desperately need you to be an anchor they can hold on to as they navigate the external pressure they face. When they know you are there, they feel secure.

If you have more than one child, chances are high that they will mature at different ages, be influenced by circumstances differently, and process experiences in different ways. They are unique people. It would be a disservice to treat them all the same. The more children you have, the more you will need to be deliberate in your observation.

GETTING SOCIAL

We are created to enjoy relationships. Some teens are more extroverted than others, but most teens need connection. Teenagers need to feel they belong somewhere. Why do you see such a draw toward social-media sites, gangs, and peer groups? Could it be that teens simply aren't getting those emotional needs met by their parents?

Taking time to cultivate closeness within the family is so important. One way you can accomplish this is by getting to know your kid's friends. We did this by being the home our kids would bring their friends to. Teens need to learn valuable social skills, and there's no better place to learn than at home with all their friends around. Some may think this is overbearing and sheltering, but I think that encouraging teens to invite their friends over is reaching out while providing opportunities for growth. Having your child's friends at your home allows you to observe behaviors and attitudes in your kid as well as others.

Having your home as a gathering place may often be inconvenient. It may require more frequent repairs and cleaning. It may restrict your privacy. However, being around your kid and their friends can have a long-lasting impact. Remember, relationships are eternal. Dirty floors, broken things, and loud evenings with little sleep are temporary. The memories made together are worth it.

We hosted New Year's Eve parties, Fourth of July cookouts, basketball shootouts, movie nights, lake days, camping trips, game nights, and any other event we could think of. You'd be surprised at how many kids would show up. Serve some food and keep the atmosphere light, and you have created the place to be. Now, you may be thinking that you don't have the money to feed forty kids, or your home isn't big enough. But you probably have enough room for a few kids, no matter the size of your pocketbook or home.

At these get-togethers, we'd determine not to hover or sit with everyone all the time; we'd visit and chat as opportunities arose. I realized many of these kids craved having someone older and maybe wiser to talk to. I sat and listened as these teens poured out their deepest hurts, trials, fears, and dreams. I wished their parents could hear their kids' hearts! Too often, these teens would say that their parents had their own struggles, were too busy, always criticized, or weren't interested in their children's problems. These conversations strengthened my personal resolve to be the parent my kids opened up to. I wanted them to know I was trustworthy. I wanted to guard my time so I'd have margin for them. Looking back, every investment of intentionality and availability was worth it.

Children are your most important ministry. You have more influence over them than over any other person in the world. If you plan to provide a sense of belonging inside the family structure, your teen will have a better chance of resisting peer pressure. Kids can and will identify with something. Their need for personal identity allows us to come alongside them, to let them know they belong to our families. The more we provide our children with a sense of family identity, the less likely they will be to seek identity elsewhere. Instead, they will learn how to have healthy, appropriate relationships with their peers—not replacements for a missing family.

TECHNOLOGY AND TEENS

There is nothing inherently wrong with technology or communicating online. In fact, many of you have close friendships with people who don't live in your city. We live in Orlando, Florida, and some of my closest friends live in Memphis, Tennessee. Thanks to FaceTime, Skype, WhatsApp, text messaging, and Messenger, we can stay connected in a way we couldn't otherwise. This is equally true of our teens. Teens think nothing of proximity where friendships are concerned.

Even though it might not always feel like it, technology is neutral. As Kathy Koch wrote in *Screens and Teens*, technology can even be life-giving. The various technologies are tools and toys—something we use to get work done, to connect with others, to plan vacations. The problem isn't technology or social media; it is how we use them. That is why we must teach our kids when and how to use them.[2]

When my children entered the teen years, technology was taking off, changing how we lived and interacted with others. There were no books to read about how to navigate this unknown, sometimes-scary world. Over time, I realized that book knowledge can only offer insights. To truly understand my children and how they would cope with constant connection and overwhelming information, I had to invest time. If you do this with your teen, your time will increase your influence. You will discover areas they struggle with or weaknesses they have to overcome.

Our kids are facing challenges unlike those from any other time in history. The Internet has changed everything. Parents are competing against every possible form of communication. Families are bombarded with devices and technology that, though useful, can undermine the work you are doing to build a close family if left unchecked. It's important to discern how to handle technology wisely with your teen in order to invest in their long-term health and your relationship with them.

According to Jim Burns, who wrote *Understanding Your Teen*, parents may make one of two mistakes when it comes to technology and social media: Either parents ignore the dangers, or they are too strict.[3]

It is easier for parents to ignore potential issues, pretending their kids will be fine, than it is to deal with the pushback from determined teenagers. After all, it takes a great deal of time and effort to stay educated and help our teens be discerning. We are up against the forces of giant tech companies who spend billions of dollars to lure our kids into spending more time on their websites. But here's the good news: Facebook or Amazon or Apple cannot outwit God. Google doesn't control the universe. God does. And he isn't going to allow a tech giant to dethrone him.

While many parents push back on technology and device usage, teaching teens how to build a positive online footprint will make them safer in the long run. Showing teens the benefits of creating a positive footprint encourages them to view social media for the good it can be in the lives of people. They learn how it can be used to run successful businesses or create a movement or support a cause—something that impassions a teenager.

Our teens are relational people. As we learn to pay attention to their needs (emotional, spiritual, physical, and relational), we can gently guide them through the maze of apps and information they are exposed to. Here are some important guidelines that will help us:

- Create defined boundaries
- Enforce consistent consequences
- Stay one step ahead
- Establish device-free times
- Plan online activities that you can play together

Phones

Have you tried to have a conversation with your teen, only to be interrupted by someone texting them—and watch them answer the text while nodding their head at you? It happens all the time. Teens pop in and out of real-life conversation repeatedly. Their friends expect a text to be answered within seconds. When I realized this was the expectation, we implemented times during the day when our children were not allowed to answer their phones. We told the kids to make sure their friends knew they would not be getting a response from them between certain hours. At first, they complained. But they had to learn to stay focused on the people they were with at the time. Surprisingly, when other parents got wind of this, they started implementing a similar policy.

Phones are useful tools. Teaching teens to use them as such puts them in control. Whether you give your teen a phone in sixth grade, eighth grade, or tenth grade, your goal should be to instill proper phone etiquette, reinforce your family phone policy, and establish phone-free zones and times. Implement morning and bedtime routines that don't include checking social-media sites, WhatsApp, or text messages; you'll help your teen get moving and connect with you in the morning and have time to think without interruption before nodding off to sleep. Teens need to learn that they will miss important things if they're always staring at a screen—an answer to a problem, a creative thought, an almost-forgotten dream. Help them learn to let technology wait a moment. They will be tethered to a device all day.

Teach them the value of letting God have a moment of their time, a moment when they're free to listen to his whisper.

Social Media

Social media is not bad. It meets our teen's need for connection and relationship. They can get minute-by-minute updates on who is in a relationship, what their friends ate for lunch, where they are hanging out on Friday night. But our teens can use technology and social media for good or evil. Our son can receive a text letting him know he's been chosen for the soccer team or sent a sext at any time. Unfortunately, we can't filter out all the bad, but we can walk alongside our teens as they learn to use devices wisely. Navigating all the social-media platforms is challenging, but there is no excuse to stay uninformed about what our teens are doing online.

We also have an opportunity to model wise social-media behavior. Some information, like how badly your fifteen-year-old is behaving or how your kid is driving you crazy, would be better to share privately with a close friend. As you set a good example of what's appropriate to post or how much time you should spend pinning photos, you will positively influence your teen.

Of course, even with your modeling, the lack of common sense about social media among teenagers is concerning. The screen deceives these young adults. The impulse to share, be seen, be noticed causes many to get into trouble. Teach them a good rule of thumb on whether to put something on social media: Is this something you'd want your parents or grandparents to see one day? Does this honor the Lord? You can also ask your teen if they'd want a future spouse to see it, or if they'd want their future children to see it. Get them to think beyond the moment.

Once, as my kids and I took a morning walk along the beach, I used our footprints behind us to talk about the impact of our actions on social media: "Just like anyone else who walks along this beach can see exactly where we've walked, anyone on social media can see the things we post. Our online lives are like a story that others read—and most of it stays visible forever."

"But the waves crash on the shore and wash away our footprints," my daughter pointed out. "Just like Snapchat automatically deletes posts."

"That's true in a sense. But even if we choose to delete an image or a post or a social-media website does that for us, the words or pictures are still somewhere in cyberspace or on a screenshot by someone else. Plus, the photos are still on our phones."

"I hadn't thought about it that way." My daughter squinted at me in the bright sunlight.

"Remember, too, God always knows where you've been. Even if you don't post a picture on Instagram."

Whether you hike or visit a beach, look for opportunities to show your teen how they leave tracks, or footprints, behind. Remind them that they can leave a trail that inspires others and honors God, or not.

People have lost contracts, jobs, and reputations—and have even been prosecuted—for social-media posts. During the teen years, use the stories that you read or the news that you hear to educate your child on the dangers of social media. Let them know how these issues and behaviors can impact their life.

I did a podcast with other social-media experts on the topic of teaching teens the importance of creating a social profile geared toward their getting into college. Our focus was to help parents understand how colleges and employers use teens' social profiles in the admissions and hiring process. It was an eye-opening experience for these parents. At that time, nearly 40 percent of colleges made their decisions based on social-media postings. When kids heard this, they were shocked. They honestly believed that what they posted would disappear in twenty-four hours.

Teens care about their future. When we teach them to view social-media postings through the lens of an employer or a school-admissions officer, they become more aware of the images they share. Help them learn the value of leaving a positive social-media footprint, one that they'll be proud of when they are older.

When your kid enters the teen years, be determined to stay one step ahead of them on social media. As a parent, you may not grasp how it all works or understand their attachment to it, but it will serve you well to try to learn more.

Bullying and Cyberbullying

Ask any teen if they know someone who has been bullied or cyber-bullied, and they will likely say yes. Bullying is at an all-time high. Your kid's life can be destroyed in 280 characters or less on Twitter, or by that picture being used against them on Snapchat. Those of us who didn't grow up in the world of social media don't think of cyberbullying the way our teens do. As Burns says, "We need to guard against insensitivity to what kids today consider a major issue."[4] The Internet has changed the way people bully others. Because of the widespread access to apps, people often pose as someone they aren't to get your kid to talk to them. Once the conversation gets started, emotional or physical harm can follow.

The issue of bullying can't be ignored. If you think it couldn't happen to your teen or that your teen wouldn't bully others, you're putting them—and yourself—at risk. What your kid does to others online can get you in a lot of trouble with law enforcement. Those practical jokes, crude comments, idle threats, or careless posts are taken seriously. Long gone are the days of "Teens will be teens." Your teen needs to understand the consequences of their actions before they make a foolish decision. And your teen needs to know what to do should they be a bully's target.

You must battle with bullying as quickly as possible. There is a strong link between bullying and suicide: "Bully victims are between 2 to 9 times more likely to consider suicide than non-victims, according to studies by Yale University. . . . 10 to 14 year old girls may be at even higher risk for suicide."[5] And bullying can take various forms: physical bullying, emotional bullying, cyberbullying, sexting, or circulating suggestive or nude photos or messages about a person.

If your teen is being bullied, chances are that they are afraid something bad is going to happen and that they can't stop it. Though cyberbullying is hard to track, do not hesitate to get involved. Your child needs your help as they navigate potentially dangerous territory.

Teens are often afraid to tell you they are being bullied out of fear of retaliation or fear of being labeled a snitch. But there are some things you can do to protect your child and empower them to seek help:

- Assure them of your desire to protect them.
- Educate yourself about the apps and devices your teen is using.
- Give your kid clear guidelines for what constitutes acceptable and unacceptable behavior.
- Remind them not to give personal information to others online.
- Don't overreact if your child tells you they are being bullied.
- Listen carefully and ask leading questions.

The Information Superhighway

When many of us parents were growing up, we didn't have the Internet, and we didn't have cell phones. In fact, we didn't have most of the digital media that we have now! However, today our kids are constantly bombarded with news, information, billboards, and seductive advertisements. As adults, we are able to process much of this and let some of it go in one ear and out the other. But teens pay attention to everything that comes across their screens.

The provocative images young people see can lead them down a path that can potentially harm them and others. The media reveals a constant bombardment of sex, seduction, and scandals. When you understand the reality your teen is facing, you're able to help them process it wisely.

There are ways you can help them deal with this information overload. First, simply don't have it around all the time. Second, have set times when they must unplug and turn off all electronics. Third, plan family activities that don't include electronic devices.

Monitor what they're watching on their computers and YouTube. Pay attention to the music they're listening to. Music has the power to influence attitudes and beliefs; that influence can be for good, but it can also influence them toward anger, violence, and identity struggles. You don't have to cut them off and restrict them from everything, but if they are engaging with unhealthy content, help them find a positive alternative. Make sure what they're watching lines up with the values you are trying to instill in them. Make sure what they're listening to is edifying and builds them up.

As a fully mature adult, you know when it's time to turn off the plethora of electronic devices. Your teen, on the other hand, does not have the same level of maturity. Their exposure to too much too young may result in increased anger, anxiety, and grief. As a parent, you have the responsibility to model self-control. It's hard, I know. But think of the cost of not teaching your child how to turn it off.

BALANCE

Our fast-paced culture is forcing us to cram more and more into our day. There are countless how-to books on work-life balance and time management, each claiming to have the secret to getting everything done. If we get a little less sleep, get up a little earlier, and work while we eat, we can stay on top of things. But we can't get everything on our to-do lists done in one day. The sooner you help your teen recognize their limitations, the easier it becomes for them to say no and set limits on their time, involvement in activities, even relationships.

Finding the right balance is not easy. It requires understanding what works for each person. This is where the time you have spent observing your teen comes in handy. Knowing how your child processes and manages life helps you guide them.

Pam, a mom in her early forties with a seventeen-year-old daughter, once approached me for help. She and her daughter, Teri, were constantly arguing over how Teri was spending her time. Teri would tell her mom she didn't understand how much Teri had to do every day. Pam was convinced Teri wasn't managing her time well. Arguing was putting a real strain on their relationship.

Over coffee one morning, I asked Pam to tell me about Teri's day.

"She has school, soccer practice four days a week and games on Saturday, piano lessons on Tuesday plus one hour of practice every day, a babysitting job three times a week, youth group on Wednesday night, and church on Sunday."

I took a sip of coffee. "When does she sleep?"

Ignoring my question, she continued, "She isn't keeping up with school assignments or chores."

"Was Teri always this busy?"

"Pretty much." Pam sighed and closed her eyes as though she finally understood. With a schedule this full, it was no surprise Teri was struggling. She was trying to squeeze far more than she could do into a week.

Parents must help their teens learn how much they put on their plates. If they don't, their teens will face greater challenges in college or in the workforce because they will overcommit and then struggle to keep up. Your teen might not appreciate having to stop doing activities they enjoy, but reiterate that your job is to coach them on how to manage their life; they will need those skills as they enter college or have a family of their own.

Parents should also be mindful of how they manage their own time. Your teen is watching! Parents are trying to juggle raising children; managing car pools, laundry, meals, and work; and spending time with their spouses. If your life is out of balance, you will have a hard time getting your teen to listen to your advice.

ENCOURAGEMENT

Encouragement is your best friend during these critical years. Your teen needs to know they are enough. When teens know who they are is enough, their confidence rises. Being encouraged to try without fear of failure empowers them to try harder. They know that no matter what, you will not think less of them.

Watch out for changes in wardrobe, hairstyle, makeup, musical preferences, friends, and attitude toward siblings or parents. These are important indicators someone else may be influencing your child. Teens will be influenced by someone or something, so I challenge you to be that someone. The greater their sense of belonging within the family, the more equipped they are to manage outside influences.

Look for ways you can encourage your child in their everyday life. Look for entrepreneurial opportunities. Teach them to use technology for good. And look for ways to express to your child their value. Tell them they are fearfully and wonderfully made (see Psalm 139:14). Show them you do understand their world.

As the years passed and I sought to understand each of my children, I stopped hearing, "Mom, you don't understand." Instead they began to say, "Mom, I know you understand. How do I handle this?" As a parent, isn't that ultimately what you want your teen to do?

If you are experiencing a broken relationship with your teen, it is never too late to make changes. This may take time and patience as you seek to gain their trust and respect. But as you seek to understand their world, you can win their heart.

WRAPPING IT UP

Ask yourself a few important questions:

- Does my teen know they matter to me?

- Have I determined to really understand what my kid is facing?

- Am I honoring the position of influence God has charged me with?

- How many other people are raising our child?

- How are technology and social media impacting my teen?

- Have I taught my kid God's Word regarding family relationships?

- Am I taking time to discover what pressures my teen is facing? Do I tell them I'm available to help?

"Mom, stop interrupting me. I'm trying to tell you a story." My daughter's voice had a frustrated tone.

"What are you talking about?" I snapped back. "I'm trying to get more details. How can I help you if I don't understand what you're saying?"

Jaclyn tightened her lips into a thin line. "You make me forget what I'm trying to say every time you interrupt me."

"But we are having a conversation." I placed one hand lightly on her shoulder.

She pulled away from my touch. "No, we aren't! I don't want you to solve my problems. I just want you to listen."

I was taken aback. Had my questions really become disruptive to her thought process? I simply hoped for an honest, intimate conversation. Obviously, my efforts weren't providing what Jaclyn needed. If I wanted to maintain a position of influence in her life, I had to learn to listen well. She wasn't trying to be disrespectful. She was letting me know she needed me to be a sounding board, not a problem solver. My parenting goal needed to change: I had to allow her to talk so she could solve her own problems.

Even though I understood the importance of listening, I had to learn *how* to listen to her. She wanted me to be there as she processed life and made sense of what was going on around her. I know how hard it is to be quiet; I'm a talker and a fixer. Tell me the problem, and I'll give you a step-by-step plan to work it out. But that day—and many others like it—I learned that most teens don't need our steps; they need a good set of ears if we want them to share what's on their hearts.

As parents, we want to take care of our children. It's natural. We've been fixing problems since they were born. But if we aren't careful, this habit can continue into the teen years. While the situations are more complex and have greater consequences, we need to let our teens try to work through issues as they arise. When Jaclyn started to tell me about her problems, I had to learn to avoid interrupting until I heard the whole story. Although our words may provide valuable information, it's not usually what's needed at that moment.

Lack of listening was the second highest complaint I heard in my years of working with teens. It caused them to be incredibly frustrated with their parents. And it was my kids' top complaint! The ironic part is that most parents, if asked, would describe themselves as good listeners.

So how does a parent bridge the listening gap? It's simple—you have to be willing to ask your teen if they feel listened to. If you have been working on having good communication, they will let you know. Sometimes they will express the need politely, and sometimes it may come up in the middle of an argument. Don't ignore what they say, even in the midst of conflict. And make time to listen.

Say *no* to scrolling through social media when your teen is around. Plan a special biweekly or monthly date night, even if all you do is go get ice cream and walk around together. Set aside time when your child can talk late at night. Give your teen permission to look away while they tell you something, knowing it doesn't mean they are being disrespectful. Consider they might not be mature enough to look you in the eye and see your reaction to their words.

Why is listening so important? Because it strengthens the relationship in a deeper way. Contrary to what many believe, buying kids anything they want and giving in to every request they make are not what ultimately win them over. They want you to listen when they need to talk. Often, teens feel as if they are being talked *at*, not talked *to*. When you pause to hear your teen's thoughts, you communicate their worth. Listening shows interest. The talker feels valued, and the listener gains useful information that helps cement the relationship. If you are committed to listening, your teen will want to come to you when something is on their mind. If you are not available or willing to listen, they will find someone who is.

Look at your teen's social-media or mobile-phone conversations. They are talking to someone. Sadly, far too many teens reach out to the wrong people in their quest to feel accepted. But it's possible to be the person your teen seeks out first. The family is the first institution the child ever knew. The bond between parent and child is unlike any other. This relationship doesn't stop during the teen years—in fact, we pray it blossoms as they grow into adults. But parents need to learn the balance of letting go while remaining connected emotionally.

Unfortunately, your child enters the teen years already having experienced broken confidences and unfaithful friendships. As a result of being hurt, ignored, or abandoned, some teens withdraw and say they don't know whom they can trust. And that includes us as parents.

I had to practice listening with all five of my children. Some of them required a little more work on my part because either they talked slowly or I would interrupt them. As the years passed, I realized my struggle to listen emerged from my fear of their messing up. I thought about everything that could happen: breaking bones, hurting someone, getting in an accident, being bullied. While it is true that teens can get into trouble, we must learn to stop controlling and overprotecting them. And we must become better listeners—not skeptics.

What are the relational advantages to listening? You gain access to your teen's world. And, when you learn about them, they feel connected to you. That connection leads to earned trust. Once you have their trust, they'll open up to you. You become a safe place for sharing fears, hopes, and dreams. This access—this "in" with your teen—gives you a chance to shape who they become as an adult.

Here are five benefits of listening to your teen:

- Listening helps you understand their thought process.
- Listening shows value and respect.
- Listening provides useful information you may use to formulate a respectful response.
- Listening teaches them to become better listeners.
- Listening earns their trust.

The act of listening encourages a teen to share without the fear of correction or judgment. When you listen, you will learn a lot about your child's motives, fears, desires, and struggles. Once you understand how your teen thinks, you can steer the conversation while guiding your teen through the decision-making process, all of which is imperative in the relationship-building stages. To feel heard, they need to know you are there for them, and nothing says that like building your relationship with them.

THE ART OF LISTENING

My oldest daughter, an artist/photographer, paints beautiful pictures. She sees things that most people miss—the expression of joy when a dog licks a child's face or the gaze of a parent who cares for a sick child. Her art reflects her heart and impacts others.

Listening is an art form. When we become proficient listeners, we empathize. We can picture tears streaming down a teen's face after her best friend makes fun of her. We can visualize her excitement when she finds out she made the track team. Those are powerful images that can strengthen your relationship.

One of my mentors once told me, "The window of time for hearing your teen's deepest secrets is short. So make the most of the time you have." I have never forgotten those words. Everyone knows how fast time passes, yet we often let a day, a week, or even a month pass without making a point to listen to the people who matter most.

If teens want to talk, then what hinders us from listening? The reasons vary: You know what's best, you have more wisdom, or they are making bad decisions. These are valid reasons, but are they enough to avoid hearing your teen? Not when you are focused on learning about them. Perhaps you are too busy or distracted, or it's bad timing—all are hindrances to listening. But it's important that you commit to making time, even if it means taking something else off your plate, to show your teen that they are more important than anything else in life.

Throughout this book, we're talking about a lot of specific areas that build closeness with your teen. However, any attempts you make can be significantly hindered if you don't model the art of listening. What does it take for your teen to want to talk to you? You guessed it—talk less, listen more!

Become a student of what your teen says, not overlooking the meaning behind their words. Think about the skilled artist who carefully paints. The artist doesn't always express exactly what is in their mind the first time. Sometimes they have to paint over a section before getting it right. And in the same way, the more the teen shares, the clearer their meaning will be. It's not uncommon for a teen to say the opposite of how they really feel when they try to express their feelings about something for the first time. No matter how much you have to bite your tongue, let your child talk about their feelings or frustrations. You'll be tempted to interject, but don't do it. Wait. Give your teen time to try again. They are angry, frustrated, or hurt, so expect them to have difficulty being clear and concise. Be patient.

In a world of nonstop chatter, you will be well served by being all ears when your child talks. The art of listening is a skill you develop over time, and you can do so if you commit and practice. But the art of listening is also an intentional act you choose to perform. How do you become an effective listener? Listen to learn, listen to resolve conflict, and recognize hindrances.

Listen to Learn

Almost all parents agree that listening is important (others feel as if their voice is the most important one in this stage of life), but few realize the valuable relational connection and information you gain from this process that puts you squarely in your teen's world.

I have always thought of myself as a good listener. My success in business depended on how well I got to know people. And I found the best way to get to know them was by asking good questions and listening carefully to their answers. Because of this, I envisioned my conversations with my teens as free-flowing. I'd ask questions; they'd joyfully respond. We would enjoy dialogue between two people who loved each other. Right?

Wrong! I found talking with friends, coworkers, basketball moms, and even the dog easier than getting some of my teens to talk. I thought,

No problem. I'll change my approach. This can't be that hard. I'd try asking the same question ten different ways. Instead of getting them to talk, I faced blank stares, crossed arms, and, of course, eye rolls.

Over time, I realized that the goal of listening was to learn *about* my kids, not so much to learn what I *could do for* my kids. While there wasn't a perfect question I could ask, there was a strategy that worked every time: Let them talk and pay attention to their point of view. It didn't matter how different my kids were from each other. If I focused on learning, they would open up and share information with me. The minute I went into fix-it or lecture mode, the conversation ended. They shut down because they felt as though I were trying to control them or, at the very least, control their situation (which, honestly, I was). My teens, like millions of others, desired to assert their independence and try handling life on their own. It wasn't my job to make sure nothing went wrong. They wanted to see that I was interested in *them* and not just in their problems.

Listening allowed me to learn about their attitudes and beliefs. It was crucial that they knew I would hear them out, regardless of the topic. I wish I could say I never interrupted or blurted out my five-step plan, but that wouldn't be true. It took time, patience, and self-control on my part. The key was to keep trying. And so should you.

I will never forget an argument between Jonathan and me over a misunderstanding. We were driving to the doctor to get his wisdom teeth extracted. He was associated with some shenanigan I heard about, and I assumed he was involved. Wanting to get to the bottom of it quickly, I went straight to accusation and blame. Well, those didn't go over very well. The more I talked, the more defensive he became. The more defensive he became, the more upset I got. It didn't take long before I was in full-blown lecture mode. I could tell by his body language that he had checked out of the conversation. Then he told me he wasn't going to keep talking if I didn't do a better job of listening. Ouch!

I knew Jonathan had the maturity to make wise decisions, but my teeny bit of doubt translated into distrust—exactly what I *didn't* want to communicate. As a result, he shut down. Once I realized what I had done, I asked him to forgive me for doubting him, which, thankfully, he did. Then I asked him if we could start over. Being humble enough to admit we're wrong encourages complete forgiveness. I was able to use lead-in questions—*What were the factors that led to the incident? What made you go along with the crowd? Did your conscience bother you?* These showed him I trusted him rather than assuming he had done something wrong.

When we listen to learn, we can discern the right questions to ask to dig deeper. We empower our teens to speak the truth and answer honestly when we ask questions that facilitate transparent responses.

Listen to Resolve Conflict

For most of us, the only time our homes are conflict-free is when no one is home or when everyone is asleep. But while complete peace and harmony might be the dream, navigating conflict constructively within the home is an opportunity for teens to learn conflict-resolution skills. And that education starts with you. You can create a home where you resolve conflicts without angry outbursts or vicious name-calling. Peace is possible. A healthy resolution must be modeled correctly and consistently, and conflict must not be pushed aside but rather brought to the forefront.

Conflicts are often the result of misunderstandings, and they're more likely to happen when we don't fully understand where the other person is coming from or we haven't let the other person speak. Learning to resolve conflict is a necessary life skill that our teens need to learn. It requires an amount of maturity and reasoning ability—and it means listening so we can respond thoughtfully to what is said.

The more intentional we are at listening—not just waiting until it's our turn to talk—the less relational conflict we will experience.

CONFLICT RESOLUTION WITH YOU

Teaching teens how to resolve disagreements with you shows them that you are humble, teachable, and interested in helping them be a part of the process and solution. The most efficient way for you to begin is to gather all the information without overreacting.

Many times, learning to work through conflict means first working through hurt feelings and pent-up resentments on their part over things such as your interjecting at the wrong time. Before you know it, a simple misunderstanding causes friction, which is followed by emotional distance. As you consider that your teen is changing and may bounce between rational and irrational comments, your ability to practice self-control during confrontation could defuse a potentially dicey situation. Your best response is no response at first. Listen before you begin to offer any type of resolution. Concentrate on what they are trying to get you to hear. Then express your willingness to sit and listen, and listen some more. Affirm how much you appreciate their coming to you. Their desire to talk grows as you show interest.

We also have to realize that teens are not going to say everything correctly. Extending grace when they lash out gives them time to settle down. This is easier to do when we accept that we don't always respond to everything correctly either. It is your job as the parent to guide them through the process. Show them how to forgive by being forgiving. Pursue reconciliation; don't wait for them to do it.

Most of all, be patient. When you do respond, speak in a way they hear and make sure you understand their point of view. Remember, they more than likely already know what you think.

Here are helpful things to keep in mind as you seek to resolve conflict with your teen:

- Don't assume you know what they are going to say.
- Take time to gather all the facts instead of rushing to judgment.
- Don't interrupt; wait until they have finished talking. If that means writing down a thought so you don't forget, then do it. Be fully attentive.
- If you forget and interrupt, be quick to apologize. And ask them to continue talking.
- Look for the hidden reason behind their frustration.
- Wait for them or you to settle down before trying to resolve the issue. A little time apart may help both of you calm down.
- Repeat what you heard them say. Often, teens don't articulate their feelings clearly. By asking them for clarity, you minimize the risk of confusion.
- Let them tell you when you've hurt or offended them. This builds trust and respect.
- Don't start your conversation by telling them what they did wrong. That immediately puts them on the defense. Ask them to tell you what happened.

It's amazing what God can do in your relationship when you are willing to practice this critical skill. Your teen may not understand what you're doing. They may question your motive at first. But know this: The conflict between you can be greatly reduced when you take time to listen to resolve it.

CONFLICT RESOLUTION WITH OTHERS

No matter how much teens try to avoid getting into conflict with others, conflicts happen sooner or later. Do you remember the time you made your best friend mad because of a misunderstanding? Or the time your friends pulled away from you, and you didn't understand why? The same thing is happening to your teen, but there is much more at stake. You didn't have social-media outlets to manage. Or text messages that many teens respond to in 1.5 seconds! And the bullying that happened in person is now magnified by dangerous, anonymous apps that most parents don't know about. Online bullying is ruining far more lives than the schoolyard bully does. Once rumors start online, they get out of control.

Your teen's ability to address conflict is a direct by-product of your example. You are your teen's most influential teacher. Your teen watches and makes mental notes as they observe you. To become more engaged in equipping your child to handle conflict, ask them questions about situations they are dealing with. As you offer reassurance that it's safe to express their thoughts to you, they will realize you are interested in their life and will feel comfortable with you.

I frequently used these questions to get my kids to open up. You might have similar ones as a springboard for your conversations:

- Have you gathered all the facts?
- How did you handle the problem when you found out?
- Did you confront any dishonesty?
- Did you try to find out if the person had something against you?
- Do you need to ask the person's forgiveness?
- What can you do to make the situation better?

We can help our teens learn how to resolve conflict with others by teaching them how to do twice as much listening as talking. Understanding this fundamental principle—that it's hard to argue with someone who isn't arguing back—is a concept they can easily grasp. If you teach your teen to be quick to hear and slow to react, you will spare them from much future rejection and heartache.

During the conversation, give them the freedom to express how they feel emotionally. Don't be alarmed if their emotions aren't what you would expect or hope for. Yes, you are teaching them how to resolve an issue with someone, but they could also be dealing with their own personal hurt. You want to be someone who supports, not someone who questions their feelings. When your teen experiences conflicts with others, show them how to do the following:

- Break down the issue accurately without inserting emotion.
- Consider areas they might have misunderstood the other person.
- Think about the other person's perspective.
- Work to make the relationship better.
- Move toward people, not away from them.

Try suggesting that your teen use these challenges to dig deep. You can help your teen to uncover what truths there might be behind someone's actions and to learn the courage it takes to rise above it all. You may also need to help them understand that they might be contributing to the problem. I'm not suggesting that being bullied is their fault—not at all! But when our kids face other kinds of conflict, we can help them learn to become better friends, classmates, employees, sons, and daughters by looking at themselves first.

If you allow your teen to blame their problems on others or avoid resolving conflict by changing friends, their ability to cultivate lasting friendships is hindered. They also miss out on personal growth that comes from learning to be humble and admitting any wrongdoing. To raise an emotionally healthy teen, you must actively work at resolving conflict with friends and your spouse. Life is comprised of people who challenge us in some way. Your child needs you to teach him how to deal with a variety of people by your example.

Recognize Hindrances

Have you stopped to consider the things that hinder you from listening to your teen? Perhaps it's busyness, hurt, or lies. You can change any negative dynamics by identifying them and choosing to address them! Learning how to manage these common issues will yield positive relational results.

You might be thinking, *Connie, I want to listen, but I can't get my son to talk to me or tell me what's wrong. Even when I ask, he says, "Nothing."* No doubt, this is frustrating. But I encourage you to specifically pray for wisdom in getting to the root cause.

I know teens might act as if they don't care—but don't be fooled. They need someone to talk to. Remember how much time they spend online? Teens are talking—a lot! But getting them to talk with you is another matter.

Over the years, some of my kids stopped communicating with me. It was hard to take. I'd ask questions only to get silence or a terse response I wasn't prepared for. I had to discern if it was me being insensitive or them being teens. To get a dialogue going, I had to examine my life. As parents, we tend to blame our kids without first thinking it may very well be how we are connecting. A hurried lifestyle may blind us to the little things we do to sabotage our own relationships. Our actions can become hindrances not just to listening but also to getting our teens to talk.

What are some of the reasons your teen doesn't talk to you? Teens have shared with me that their parents

- Are too busy
- Don't approve of them
- Don't listen
- Show by their actions it's never a good time to talk
- Talk at them, and it always turns into an argument

- Get mad
- Correct them in the middle of a story
- Don't care

Has your teen said any of these to you? I think my kids have told me all of these things at one time or another. When they think I am not listening due to reasons like these, our communication shuts down. None of us want barriers in our relationships, and yet we continue to do the things our parents did to us that we don't want to do. How can we break the cycle? Let's look at a few of the hindrances in a bit more depth.

BUSYNESS

Paul and I had a difficult year when he was seventeen. One day, I got a call from a friend who wanted to offer her support and encouragement. She had experienced a similar situation with her son and knew what I was going through. She started talking about her experience, which made me feel comfortable sharing my struggles. As I spoke, I could hear sounds in the background. I knew she was still on the line, but I could tell she was multitasking. We are busy people who try to do more than one thing at a time. I've done it too. But I couldn't help feeling a twinge of awkwardness. Was I one of the items on her checklist for the day? I knew she cared, but I didn't feel as if she did. I understood she wanted to reach out amid her hectic mom day, but I could tell she wasn't entirely present.

The same was true for my son. When he called to talk, I'd try to do other things while he told me about class. He could sense I wasn't really available to listen. I went through the motions, but he knew when I wasn't fully present. He needed me to slow down and give him my full attention. I've learned over the years that when I focus on my kids, they talk more freely.

Teens want to feel secure in the relationship before they will tell you what's on their minds. And nothing communicates security more than the gift of time.

If you sense your schedule is out of balance, take an evening to list practical steps you can take to slow down. There is nothing noble about being too busy. You will not get a reward for being overcommitted or overachieving. Your teen will grow up to tell you how much they needed you during a crisis, but they couldn't interrupt your busy life. Or worse, your child won't tell you, but you'll sense or see a distance between you. I don't say this to heap guilt on you. But I want to challenge you, to encourage you to think about what's most important in life.

How many of us give our teens just enough attention to make them think we are listening? We are engrossed in something, and they interrupt us, wanting to talk about random topics—a friend stopped texting them, they missed getting an A on an exam by one question, they are stressed about an upcoming test. These conversations may appear insignificant, but they matter greatly to your teen. And these seemingly unimportant conversations become building blocks for your future relationship with your child. Give them your undivided attention.

I'm not saying that whenever your teenager needs you, you have to drop everything so you can listen. Or that not being available the moment they wish to talk to you will cause harm. But your availability strengthens your relationship.

There are several things you'll want to ask yourself as you stop to listen to your teen:

- Is it urgent?
- Is someone hurt?
- Can it wait until later in the day?
- Is there something I should do to help?

Once you've answered these questions, assess a plan of action. What do you need to do right now? When can you carve out one-on-one time? How much time do you need? Can this be handled in one sitting, or do you need a few late-night conversations? Knowing if your teen is long-winded, dramatic, logical, introverted, extroverted, easily hurt, or quick to anger helps you plan your course of action. Stop and think about what they need from you and how you can help them work through the situation.

There will be moments when your teen is fearful or hurting and you will have the chance to stop what you are doing to listen. Don't let your busyness become a roadblock that pushes them away. Listening with your full attention will make them want to come to you when future situations arise.

HURT

A hurt or wounded spirit can become a roadblock to getting your teen to talk or listen to you. Often, hurt arises because of hurtful words—the words our teens say to us or we say to our teens.

For years, I heard a teenager named Daphne make comments about her father's critical remarks when she tried to talk to him. Most of the time, her comments were subtle, but anyone could sense that her hurt came from a deep, vulnerable place. Every conversation with her father left her emotionally drained.

During one of our conversations, I asked Daphne if her father spoke to other family members in the same way. I was trying to understand if the two of them had a personality clash I could help her work through. But, sadly, he did talk to others critically as well. Every time family members tried to talk with her dad, he would put them on the defensive with his comments. She said that after twenty years of marriage, her mother learned to tune him out. Whenever he became upset, her sister, wanting to show respect, lingered until he finished talking but would usually start crying. Daphne, on the other hand, would quietly get up and walk out of the room, hoping to escape without being dragged into the conversation. She'd hide in her room or escape to the front porch. Staying away proved less painful. Much like her mother, she did not want to be on the receiving end of the verbal exchange.

Daphne longed to be heard by her father. Because he failed to listen, their relationship was strained. Was it all his fault? Some of it was, of course, but fault is rarely one-sided. There is a shared breakdown somewhere, and there is a mutual responsibility to work things out. For Daphne and her father, healing took some time, but he eventually apologized for not wanting to hear her side of things and for his reaction. She learned how to control her temper, and he learned how to listen. Daphne and her father worked toward a mutually beneficial relationship and, thus, experienced a positive change in their relationship and the family dynamic. But their story could have ended in ruin without a shift in how they interacted.

Ask yourself the following questions to make sure you are not hurting your child:

- Did I stop to think before reacting?
- Were my words cutting or sarcastic?
- Was I being unreasonable?
- Did I apologize?

With these questions in mind, you'll want to make sure you remove any barriers to your hearing them or their hearing you. If you've said things that have hurt your teen, make it right.

No loving parent wants to experience a broken relationship with their teen. And they don't have to. Parents are well served when they listen and control their tongues. Strife and heartbreak are not always possible to avoid, but the healing power of humility and listening removes many of the hindrances parents face. We need to remember the goal is to keep the hearts of our teens, not to win every confrontation.

LOCATION

Have you been in public when your son or daughter brought up a sensitive topic? While we might blush, the presence of others doesn't seem to faze our teens. Thanks in part to social media, kids are losing their inhibitions. People laugh at their posts and share them on Snapchat, and all their friends think they're funny. So what should you do when they bring up inappropriate comments in public? How does this affect your ability to listen to what they want to talk about if the location isn't conducive to deep conversation?

As a parent, you get to help your teen be discerning. Your gentle guidance goes a long way when they're learning to say what's appropriate at the right time and what comments should be discussed privately. They will learn it's better to discuss certain topics when others can't listen in.

Teens live in a culture where almost all topics are fair game, and there are very few taboo issues. Their world is very different from when you were a teen. It used to be that girls would talk about things among themselves that they would never discuss with boys, and boys would do likewise. However, that has changed, and teens of both sexes talk about almost anything in front of each other.

You can be prepared for an awkward conversation with these questions:

- Do we need to talk about the topic at the soonest possible time?
- Do I make light of what they say in public?
- Have I explained the importance of being discreet?

The lines of what to say and when to say it are not as clear-cut these days. Teens witness adults saying awful things in public and online. Conversations we once expected adults, especially those in leadership, to have in private rarely happen that way. Instead, people feel empowered and entitled to air their dirty laundry in front of the world. This culture makes teaching teens harder, as they are confused by the mixed messages. But we still need to help our teens learn what appropriate public conversation is and what should be discussed in private.

Here are some questions you can ask your teen to help them discern between public and private topics:

- Does this need to be said right now?
- Will saying this be tearing another person down?
- Will this information hurt someone?
- Would this person be bothered by my discussing this topic?
- Will this information make anyone feel uncomfortable?
- Is this better shared in a one-on-one context?
- Is this better shared only with a safe person like a parent or trusted teacher?

LIES

One night at our home, a group of teens sat around a bonfire, talking about things they had lied to their parents about. I was very interested in what they had to say, so I quietly sat as they spoke. After listening for a while, I asked them why they felt they needed to lie. They quickly spouted a list of reasons. These were *good* kids who came from good homes. They'd been taught that lying is wrong. Their willingness to be open helped me understand their point of view.

I know lying is not acceptable in your home—it wasn't in ours. But teens commonly don't know how to handle a situation and therefore resort to lying.

Lies make us angry, and they erode our trust. Lying even causes some parents to get so upset that they lose control and become angry.

But when our teens lie to us, there is often a hidden message we need to understand. Teens lie for many reasons:

- They are afraid of how we might view them or how we might react.
- They want something so badly or dislike something so much that they are willing to do almost anything to get their way.
- They are embarrassed by the truth or fear the consequences.
- It's easier than telling the truth, as in the case of telling an acquaintance they simply can't go to the movies because they don't like that person and want to avoid hurting their feelings.

Teens often call these "little white lies." Whatever the reason for lying, we need to teach our teens to be honest. When we teach them how to handle sticky situations well, they earn God-honoring character qualities in the process. Remind them a person who lies about small things will lie about bigger issues.

Because they are maturing, some teens lie when they feel trapped, and sometimes we parents are the ones doing the trapping. Once, when I suspected one of my kids wasn't being honest, I backed him into a corner. He had no place to go. If he told the truth, he'd be in trouble, and if he lied, he'd be in trouble. It wasn't fair to him, and it strained our relationship. Though I had good intentions—not allowing my child to get away with lying to me—I used an ineffective method. I should have asked leading questions without provoking my son. Doing so would have defused a tense situation and helped us both get to the truth.

Backing our teens into a corner creates a fight-or-flight response. Neither of these reactions creates open, honest communication. To avoid putting your child on the defensive, don't ask them questions that you already know the answer to. Let them know you want to guide them through this situation; don't make it more difficult for them to tell you the truth. If they lied to save face, help them learn how to handle those awkward social situations appropriately. Unless there is a regular pattern of lying, use these moments to equip your teen with the courage to be truthful, even if it means not getting what they want.

Because we want to raise honest kids, we might tend to overreact when we discover that our children didn't tell us the truth. Rather than confront your teen when they lie, push the reaction-pause button first. Use this as an opportunity to guide them to be truth tellers in a society where truth is not always encouraged.

TIME

We have a family tradition of watching Christmas movies together. One of our favorites is *Elf*. I pay close attention to two characters: Walter Hobbs, the dad, who is a publishing executive in NYC, and his son Michael, a young teen who desperately wants a relationship with his dad. Throughout the movie, you see the tension rise between these two characters. Because his dad works all the time, Michael feels unloved and disconnected. In a climactic scene, Michael bursts into an important meeting and confronts his dad. Walter is faced with a choice: lose his job or lose his son's heart. He stares at Michael, then at his boss, and then looks away, as if to consider the impact of his decision. Those seconds are riveting. Finally, he turns back to his boss and quits his job.

It is easy to get caught up in other activities and ignore our teens' need for our time. There are times when life demands more of our attention, but those times can't be ongoing. Not if you want to build the relationship you are after.

Listening requires time. Time doesn't find you; you find time. As you go about your day—cleaning up after dinner or driving home from practice—look for the opportunity to ask your teen a question or two. Something as small as getting a glass of water from the fridge when your son is in the kitchen or sitting in your daughter's room as she gets ready for an evening with friends can invite dialogue. Your teen will be glad you started the conversation. They want to hear from you, even if they don't act like it.

Don't expect your teen to just jump into a deep conversation. They may have to test the waters a little, especially if you've been a little preoccupied. Try asking leading questions that require more than one-word answers:

- How is your friend doing with (insert problem)?
- What happened at (insert event)?
- What are you going to do about (insert issue)?

Meaningful conversations usually start with unimportant questions. Lighthearted conversations put your teen at ease and build a closer relationship. They can take place anywhere, and these questions can get your teen to talk, which is what you want. Deeper and more meaningful conversations can happen once they start talking with you.

I know this all sounds easy—you listen, they follow. But I understand what you're up against. Everything around them teaches disrespect for parents, authority, and sometimes life itself. In the face of this prevalent attitude of disrespect, we can make intentional choices to counter the narratives of the world and build a healthy listening relationship with our children.

What we do either helps or hinders our relationships. When we listen well, our relationships thrive. When we don't listen, or we listen halfheartedly, we frustrate them. Your investment now in becoming a great listener could save you heartache later. Remember, you only have a few years with your teen, so make the most of this time by learning to listen.

WRAPPING IT UP

- What are the five benefits of listening to your teen?

- What can you do to make sure your teen knows you are fully listening?

- Does your teen see you model honesty? If not, ask the Lord to help you practice kind truth telling so your teen learns how to avoid lying.

- Ask your teen how you can be a better listener.

Chapter 8

MONITOR YOUR MOUTH

WHY DID I SAY THAT TO HER? I chided myself as my daughter walked away with tears in her eyes. I should have known better. I knew she hadn't heard what I was trying to say. All she heard was a list of words that communicated, "You aren't enough. Let me tell you how to handle this."

This kind of scenario happens in every family. As parents, we think we are saying one thing, but our teens hear something completely different. How do we make our words good for others to hear?

Communicating well and with intent begins with being slow to speak. In the last chapter, we discussed the importance of listening to our teens. To have a relationship, we must also learn how to speak—and how to read nonverbal cues—so that our teens hear the message of love through our words.

Our words generally do one of two things: build up our teens with confidence or cause great hurt and separation. The latter often shakes their confidence and wounds their spirits. Most teens aren't capable of fully sorting out what is truth and what isn't. They take it all in, every single word—the helpful, the harsh, the hurtful.

My family of origin didn't spend much time thinking about how to say something. Instead, they said what was on their minds. They made comments like "You just need to be told like it is" or "If you get your feelings hurt, well, you'd better toughen up."

As a child, I found myself running to the aid of the wounded, attempting to repair the damage inflicted through words. It wasn't that the person was innocent of wrongdoing but that they didn't deserve being spoken to harshly. As a teen, I often thought about how much words mattered, how greatly they impacted the receiver. I longed for different words—thoughtful, kind, understanding words—to come out of the mouths of my parents and other authority figures.

Words have a way of rolling off the tongue and falling directly into a child's heart. If only people could learn how to monitor their mouths before they blurt out words that have the potential to inflict pain. What if we stopped to consider how we'd want to be corrected or encouraged? What if we took a few moments before we started that conversation to see things from the other person's perspective, to consider the impact and effect of our words—so the conversation wouldn't end in tears or discouragement?

Bottom line: Our mouths need to have a filter. If you want to cultivate a healthy relationship and keep the heart of your teen, you can't just blurt out everything that comes to mind. That simply will not work.

After that conversation with my daughter, I knew I needed to be a better listener—but the situation between us had come to the point where it had to be addressed. It's a dilemma each of us will face with our children. How do we speak so our teens listen and understand? We need to start by monitoring our mouths! It's not always what you say but *how* and *when* you say it that matters.

Our teens' ages, circumstances, and personalities all play a role in discerning what to say and when to say it. When I was younger, if my parents scolded me for anything, I would melt into a puddle of tears. I took every word to heart. Because I hated getting in trouble, I watched what others did and tried to avoid making the same mistakes. My goal? To please my parents and stay out of trouble. My brother, on the other hand, talked back in defiance. The more he talked back, the worse the arguments got. He wasn't going to let anyone get away with speaking their mind, not unless he was free to speak his—which he began to do, loudly and regularly. I watched their frequent verbal battles.

Was I not brave enough to talk back, or was my brother not wise enough to be quiet? Neither. We're different people. While he appeared tough and unscathed by words of correction, he was just as vulnerable on the inside as I was. He managed to act as if words didn't hurt him. But I knew they did. Five years younger than my brother, I couldn't hide my emotions.

Your child might act as if what you say doesn't matter, but don't be fooled. Their confidence will be shaken—or increased—by what you say and how you say it.

On many occasions, words have slipped out—words that could never be taken back—before I could consider their potential impact on the listener. Even though I asked for forgiveness, the stinging bite of those words wounded one of my children, the very thing that a loving parent does not want to do. When I intentionally focus on monitoring my mouth, I become aware of the words I choose to speak.

When we don't control the words that come out of our mouths, we hurt the relationships we long for and unintentionally model a pattern our kids will one day use to parent their children. This very thought made me change how I spoke to my kids during their teen years. Monitoring your mouth means guarding what you say. I love Paul's advice on the topic: "Let your speech always be gracious, seasoned with salt, so that you may know how you ought to answer each person" (Colossians 4:6). Every parent must develop this skill because it's not something that comes naturally to most people. But it is essential to raising healthy teens. We parents typically end up talking *at* our kids, not *with* our kids. This is especially true when conflict is present. To learn to monitor your mouth, the first skill to master is gathering as much information as possible. Follow this by responding in love instead of in anger. Learning to do this well takes practice, study, discipline, and perseverance. And from that foundation, you can develop the skills needed for healthy two-way communication with your teen: being available, watching your words, asking the right questions, focusing on their needs, breathing life, communicating worth, treating them as a young adult, asking for forgiveness, resolving conflict, and reading body language and nonverbal signals effectively.

BE AVAILABLE

Your teen is less interested in your ability to say the right thing and more concerned with your availability to talk. They don't expect you to be perfect, just accessible. Like all humans, teenagers are designed for relationship. They want to be heard and validated. They have something they want to say, and they want you to be the person who listens to them.

I encourage you to work on engaging your teen, not dismissing them. The moment you respond in anger or disappointment, you've ended the conversation. They won't reveal their secrets and struggles to you. Your approval and praise matter to them; they crave an encouraging word from you.

When they share what's going on in their lives, you know how to pray for them, how to encourage them, and how to love them. Observe your teen so you can recognize when they want to talk to you about their day. Do they open up right after school when they drop their backpacks and head to the kitchen for a snack? Do they need time to refresh and relax for a few minutes after school, but they're ready to share at dinnertime? Do they prefer to chat at 10:00 p.m., when they're settling down for the night and thinking about the day? Be available and prepared to listen during the times your teen is most comfortable sharing. When you sense they want to talk, intentionally monitor your words. Also, put away your smartphone and iPad, and look them in the eyes while they're sharing about their day.

WATCH YOUR WORDS

After working all day at your job or at home, you walk into the kitchen, only to see dirty dishes everywhere. The first thing that comes out of your mouth is "Why can't anyone ever clean the kitchen?" There's a not-so-hidden implication in your question that immediately puts everyone in the house in a defensive mind-set. They think Mom's going to scold the person who messed up her kitchen.

Believe me, I understand the frustration! But there's a much bigger issue at stake here: your child's willingness to open up to you. Always try to keep your relationships in mind and love your family unconditionally. When you see your kitchen's a mess, try saying, "Wow, it looks like you had a great dinner!" They know the kitchen's not clean. But try not to start off your conversation by putting everybody on the defensive. When you do that, your child will become angry with you; an angry response doesn't show care for the people who might have enjoyed a wonderful time making dinner together, sitting around the table, and telling stories about their day. Because you relegate any relational aspect of that evening to the realm of dirty dishes, you may cause them to shut down completely. Nobody enjoys living under the burden of ongoing guilt trips.

Now, of course you should teach your child to clean up, do their laundry, wash and change their sheets, and do other chores that prepare them for life on their own. Look for ways to speak those truths in ways that show you are helping them. Does this take more time? Absolutely. But it's much more effective than barking out a bunch of rules and asking, "Why did you do this?" and "Why don't you do that?" Who wants to be around the kind of mom who walks into a room throwing verbal accusations at everyone?

You want your kid to be excited to see you. You long for them to tell you about the fun they had making dinner or the hilarious conversation they had around the kitchen table. Don't give that opportunity up for dirty dishes. Don't miss those moments because your teen didn't do everything quite right. You can teach responsibility once they've seen that you care about them. Don't let the people you love most become entangled with the situation. The two are completely separate—learn to address them separately. You'll have more harmony in your relationships, and your family will delight when they see you instead of being afraid because they didn't do the fifteen things you think they probably should've done before you got home.

We want to make sure our words edify our children, build deeper relationships, and encourage their hearts. Relationships with family members last forever. Dirty dishes and unfulfilled to-do lists do not.

ASK THE RIGHT QUESTIONS

I received a message from a woman who needed help with approaching her daughter. She explained the situation and immediately jumped to worst-case conclusions. After she finished talking, I asked her a few questions: "Has your daughter done this before?" "Does she know that you know?" "What do you want to communicate?" Before we rush into judgment, we need to stop and think about our goals. There are ways to get the information we need without driving a wedge.

Sometimes you need to gather the facts before responding to a situation. Getting your teen to share information is best accomplished by asking the right questions. Before jumping into a host of questions, get your conversation off to a good start:

- Deal with hurt or angry emotions before you engage in conversation.
- Plan a time to talk that's free from distractions.
- Think about your goal. Are you trying to discover something about your teen, resolve a misunderstanding, or share concern about an activity they're involved in?
- Don't accuse.
- Don't interrogate.
- First, affirm what they are doing right.
- State the situation you want to address.
- Explain why you need clarification.
- Listen, listen, listen.
- Keep calm.
- Forgive, restore, and reconnect.
- Agree on a plan. This usually requires some type of compromise.

We can encourage our children by learning to ask the right questions—at the right time. When you monitor your mouth, the words you speak will be well-timed because you can choose to be discerning. You want the words you speak to your kid to communicate, "I love you, and I'm here to help" and "What can I do for you?"

FOCUS ON THEIR NEEDS

Our children Jonathan and Jaclyn experienced test anxiety and as a result didn't test well, something we didn't learn until their high-school years. I had a choice to make. I could focus on the so-called deficit and say, "Try harder, try harder," or I could focus on knowing they were doing the best they could. They wanted to be like everyone else—study, take a test, and earn an A—but that didn't come naturally or easily. In this situation, I had to purposefully say, "I know this is a struggle for you, but I know you're doing the best you can. How can I help you do better?"

When we identify with our children's needs, we show grace and empathy. When we choose to ask intentional questions about what they're going through and how we can help, they are drawn toward relationship with us. In essence, we are saying, "We're in this together. I'm here for you. I want to help you. I can't fix everything, but I can do this." Teens aren't asking us to solve their problems. They need to know they aren't alone.

BREATHE LIFE

Our children gain a sense of confidence when we speak encouraging words. If we're not careful, our words can make them feel worse—as if they don't measure up. We can exasperate them to the point where they give up. They quit trying because if Mom and Dad aren't their biggest cheerleaders, they don't believe they can do anything. Their strength and confidence come from our support and encouragement.

Breathing life into our kids is more about asking ourselves whether we speak words to them that are truthful and encouraging or we make snarky comments like "Hey, I'm just saying it like it is." Most times, we don't need to say it like it is. Our parental words need to be coated with grace and love. The truth can be spoken in a compassionate way.

COMMUNICATE WORTH

Monitoring your mouth involves letting your kid dream big. Just because you didn't accomplish something doesn't mean they can't.

Don't cast your failures or your inabilities on them and hinder them from trying because of your fears. At the same time, don't try to live out your dreams through them, pushing them to do something that isn't their passion. You want them to discover who they are created to be! Be the encourager who says, "Fly! Fly big. Fly hard. Give it your best. It may not work, but give it your best." Don't push them to do what the world defines as success. Not all teens desire a certain standard of living or a job or career that is esteemed more highly than others. Encourage them to follow where God is leading them. Encourage them to do their absolute best, whatever that may be.

TREAT YOUR CHILD AS A YOUNG ADULT

It's time to start treating your teen as a young adult, not a child.

God's Word says that when you were a child, you spoke like a child, but when you grew up, you put away childish things (see 1 Corinthians 13:11). God tells us to be grown up in our youth. There's no time in Scripture where he places the teen years in their own compartment. That's a modern phenomenon. In years past, cultures recognized childhood and adulthood, and childhood ended roughly in the teen years. Kids were expected to become young adults. They worked hard to contribute to the well-being of their families—some started apprenticeships, and others worked alongside their fathers in the family business or their mothers in managing the home.

Recently, culture has begun to make excuses for this time. Parents say, "Oh well, that's just the teenage years," as if we have no real expectations for our children's lives. "They're a teenager" is used as an excuse for anything foolish they might do. That attitude and approach is simple, not biblical. God does not give teenagers free rein to do whatever they want. They are to put away childishness and become grown up in their youth.

How do we treat teens as adults?

- Stop micromanaging
- Show them respect
- Speak kindly
- Honor who they are
- Avoid responding with sarcasm
- Be quick to listen
- Give them appropriate freedoms
- Expect truthfulness
- Allow them to fail without criticism

It's easy to frustrate your teen if you keep treating them as you did when they were younger. Because of the changes happening to their body, they naturally want to begin assuming responsibility and transition into adult life. We can't treat our kids at this age the way we treated them in their elementary years, with time-outs, unbending rules, and other methods we used to get our children to obey us. That would cause a different set of problems. We make obedience attractive by showing trust, honor, and respect. If your teen stumbles, help them up and start over.

ASK FOR FORGIVENESS

Teens have a way of getting a negative reaction out of us. And my kids seemed to instinctively know how to upset me. I would love to tell you I never yelled at my kids or said hurtful comments, but that wouldn't be true. I blew it with each one of them. When I did, I'd get so down on myself because I said I'd never respond poorly. Three healing sentences instantly rolled off my tongue: "I was wrong. I am sorry. Please forgive me." When you mess up as a parent, admit it. Ask your kid for forgiveness.

In our family, we discovered how important it was for our children to say "I forgive you" after we asked for their forgiveness because we wanted them to lay down their resentment and anger. In turn, we verbally offered forgiveness to them because we wanted them to come to us and admit, "I'm sorry, please forgive me" when they'd done something that showed a lack of respect.

Forgiveness is one of the most important aspects of a healthy family. If you are honest about the fact that you have imperfections and make mistakes, your child will also confidently ask for forgiveness when they make a mistake. The road back to a healthy relationship is admitting wrongdoing and restoring the relationship by requesting forgiveness.

Sometimes you'll say something without thinking because you're having a bad day or just don't feel your best. Maybe you had an argument with your spouse, or your boss gave you a hard time, and you loathe the idea of dealing with your kid as well. But you model humility when you admit that you were wrong to speak that way. Offer an apology, and resolve to be careful with what you say in the future. Teach your child to be careful and acknowledge that they can also do damage with their tongue.

Words can destroy and wound people, sometimes beyond what they can handle. Thoughtless comments can be devastating and heart-wrenching. Your words can inflict wounds on your kid, and those wounds take time to heal. When you cross the line and offend and hurt your child, simply apologizing doesn't erase the hurt. Hurtful words are like a voice message they replay. They can hear that comment over and over in their mind. But your willingness to repent, to make amends, and to reach out and love them helps erase that message. You must do this purposefully. It's not going to come easily for you, but it's worth the effort to develop a deeper relationship with your teen.

RESOLVE CONFLICT

At times, conflict is inevitable. One or both of you say hurtful words out of frustration or anger. Maybe your child has been sassy one too many times, or you've pushed them to their limit. Parenting in the teen years is really like a beautiful dance—you learn how to work together and communicate with one another. When dancing, one leads, and the other follows. Sometimes toes get stepped on; sometimes one or the other doesn't lead well or follow properly. But with time, you both learn.

When your child makes a comment or a poor decision that hurts a family member, you need to go through a specific process to move toward healing. Don't belabor the offense. The right approach is to be slow to speak; pray first, think about what you're going to say, and think about *how* you should say it, so your teen can hear what you're saying. The most important thing is for your child to know the motivation behind your words.

When an eruption or collision occurs, and you know you're so emotionally charged that one of you will say something hurtful to the other, you may need to step away for a while. As parents, we know how to deliver cutting remarks a little better because we've had time to practice. Teens don't have that craftiness, so they often say things a little more harshly. When you're engaged in that type of conflict, tell them it's time to stop until emotions settle down. Suggest the following: "Let's take some time for ourselves, and then we'll talk about this again. I'm not sure how long you're going to need, and I'm not sure how long I'm going to need, but right now this is not helpful to either of us. We're going to say something that might hurt each other. That's not the best way to resolve conflict." This firm-yet-kind response will often defuse the situation. But if it doesn't, and your teen refuses to leave the room, it might be better for you to leave the room.

As you approach conflict in this way, your kid will start to realize that your priority is the relationship. You can reinforce that by saying, "I want a relationship with you. This is what we're aiming for. We're doing life together, and I know we don't want to keep doing it like this."

God expects many things of us parents. He expects us to pursue a right relationship with him first, and then with our children. He expects us to teach truth to our children. He expects us to be our children's greatest cheerleaders.

God also has expectations of our children. He expects them to honor us (see Exodus 20:12). He expects them to listen to what we have to say.

Amid conflict, we have a choice in how we respond. One response allows the relationship and conversation to continue, and the other basically shuts everything down. The critical thing to remember is to think beyond the words you might want to say to instead say something that allows willingness and open dialogue to develop.

NOTICE NONVERBAL LANGUAGE

We've spent time learning how our relationships with teens are affected by our words and how we need to listen to what they have to say. Now let's talk about the silent messages you and your teen communicate through body language. Body language is a powerful expression of emotions that teens haven't fully mastered yet. (Incidentally, neither have most adults.) But what we say with our body language is a critical principle to learn and apply ourselves and to teach to our children.

Body language is the first barometer children learn. They read quickly whether you seem approachable, sincere, and relatable. And the way you communicate through this silent language is a precursor to getting teens to open up.

Learning to understand and use body language to build your relationship is a powerful communication tool for showing love to your child.

When I worked for a large entertainment company, there was a sign hanging up for employees to see as they exited wardrobe: "Smile; it's a nice reflection of you." Every time I read it, I smiled. It was automatic. As I saw it day after day, year after year, the words stuck with me. Over time, I began educating others on the importance of a good first impression. The phrase "People don't care how much you know until they know how much you care" is true. The more I intentionally greeted people with a smile and a cheerful greeting, the more responsive they were to me.

Once I started having children, I realized my children responded the same way everyone else did. When I smiled at them before reacting to a situation, they were less defensive. If I smiled at them for no reason other than to communicate their importance to me, they were happier to see me. They, in turn, learned to exchange pleasantries with others, but more importantly, they learned they were worthy of being treated nicely—even if they were grumpy, discouraged, or out of sorts.

A well-timed head tilt, gentle touch, or smile conveys so very much; these gestures can even heal. Think about that time you were disappointed you didn't make the team, and your friend came up and hugged you. Or the time your grandmother gave you a warm smile and said, "Good job." Or the time your mom tilted her head while resting her hand on her chin as she listened to you talk about your best friend's birthday party. These sincere gestures made you feel loved.

What does your body language communicate? If your first response is a frown or look of disappointment or disgust, your teen reacts by building an emotional wall. This wall will remain until they sense it's safe to take it down. If this becomes your pattern, you will have to work much harder to get into your teen's world.

If you're trying to foster better communication, avoid nonverbal cues on this list. Don't

- Shrug your shoulders
- Rub your eyes with your fingers
- Shake your head in disbelief
- Breathe rapidly

- Cross your arms
- Turn away
- Drum your fingers
- Shake your leg
- Slam the door
- Block your eyes with your hands
- Wring your hands
- Point your finger
- Throw your arms up in the air
- Squint your eyebrows
- Purse or compress your lips
- Walk out of the room[1]
- Invade personal space
- Engage in piercing eye contact
- Place your hands on your hips

Conversely, the following gestures communicate interest and care. Do

- Smile as you listen
- Rest your hands in your lap or on a table
- Make eye contact
- Tilt your head
- Breathe calmly
- Relax your eyebrows

Can you picture yourself eradicating the don'ts and implementing the dos from these lists? With practice, you certainly can. And you'll be amazed at how your teen responds. Of course, even with your herculean efforts to effectively communicate nonverbally, your child still won't be perfect. But because you are intentionally showing unconditional kindness, you'll keep the lines of communication open.

WATCH YOUR RESPONSE

If you think your sweet child would never say something wrong, you're not being realistic. Sometimes they will say or do something that hurts your feelings. Your reaction reveals more about your character—or lack of it—than your teen's. They learn from your example. It isn't necessary to respond with angry outbursts. Parents should exhibit self-control. I know that isn't easy to do when children are disrespectful. I know how hard it is to not come back with a sarcastic comment or two. When our teens say hurtful words, it hurts. But I challenge you to look at the motive behind what was said and examine the circumstances that led to it. What part did you play in how the situation unfolded? Did you exasperate your child by your words or actions? This exercise isn't about placing blame. Instead, it helps you examine whether you said or did something that brought out this resentment, bad attitude, or action in your child. If your answer is *yes*, then resolve it. Focus on how you can help your teen realize they hurt you and how that hurt affects the closeness of your relationship. How can you help them learn to care genuinely? Help them understand the seriousness of their words or actions.

When these situations happened in my family, we asked our children where those hurtful actions or words came from, giving them the opportunity to tell us what was going on. Were they struggling with something related to us? Or did they just feel safer directing their frustrations toward us? Your teen may feel comfortable saying something hurtful to you, but not someone else—as they would not get away with it. Teens are smart enough to know they can be themselves at home and let their guard down. Their friends don't put up with temperamental outbursts.

Does this mean we allow our young adults to say whatever they want? No! But it does mean that we show intentionality and care in how we respond to our children.

So pay attention to the words you use. As a parent who loves and cares for your child, speak words of affection, affirmation, and approval. Say them out loud. In texts. In notes. In public. In private. Whenever possible, underscore your words with physical touch. Do it often. And though your kid might roll their eyes or give weak hugs, those expressions will not be lost on them. It is hard to resist a gentle, nurturing, caring, desirous, self-sacrificing heart.

We love our children because God loves them. We love them— even on those days when they are anything but lovable. Our time is limited. So as much as possible, we must use our words to speak life into our teens, monitoring our mouths and controlling our body language. When we do, we are modeling love and grace in a way they will remember.

WRAPPING IT UP

- What are your priorities? Do you think your teen might feel as if they're competing for your time?

- What can you lay down for a little while to free up more time for your teen?

- Where is the best place to have conversations without distractions? How can you establish device-free talk time with your teen?

- What words breathe life into your child?

- Is there something you've said you need to apologize for? Have you made amends for the words spoken out of frustration? Give your relationship a fresh start through being willing to say "I'm sorry" and ask for forgiveness.

Chapter 9

TACKLE
TOUGH TOPICS

I RECEIVED AN URGENT CALL from a friend. A mutual friend's fifteen-year-old daughter was in crisis.

"What? Who are you talking about?"

Then—

"Wait a minute. She is only fifteen years old."

And—

"What do you mean they found her in another state?"

I was completely caught off guard. Once I gathered my thoughts and settled down, we started over.

Our friend's daughter had met a man online. By posing to be about her age, he managed to lure her away.

Thankfully, authorities found her alive and returned her to her home. But the story could have had a tragic ending.

Stories like this happen far too often. We think our kids are safe, but they aren't. The Internet has changed the landscape of how evil people prey on our teens. Teens gain access to the world through technology, but they aren't savvy or equipped enough to spot danger.

We are raising teens in a world and culture where they'll be faced with all sorts of troubling situations and choices. Teens need to belong and fit in, which makes them easy targets for unscrupulous people who don't care about values or faith. Teenagers are impressionable and easily influenced, and they adopt values, attitudes, and behaviors from those around them.

Nothing paralyzes a parent more than the fear of not knowing how to mention and discuss sensitive topics. But if your teen doesn't talk to you, they will talk to someone else. You have limited time and opportunities to shape how they think about their world. You must be faithful day in and day out to equip your teen with the knowledge and understanding to navigate the issues at hand—and to model what healthy behavior and perspectives look like. Only when your teenager feels that you unconditionally love them and want their best will you have the influence that you should.

TALKING TOGETHER

Natural curiosity, the pressure to conform, and a desire to push the limits are but a few of the reasons teens engage in risky behavior. They hear about something intriguing, and then a friend invites them to try it. "It's only one time." "No one will know." "It will be fun." "All the cool kids are doing it." These persuasive tactics are successfully used every day to get your teen to say *yes*. Many times, it happens before they even have time to consider if it's right or wrong. When you are prepared to discuss tough topics, you help your teen stand strong when temptation arises.

I know it's awkward to ask your teen about what they are doing. Even pointing out what others are engaged in can be tricky. Teens get defensive when they think we are singling out one of their friends.

But talking about sensitive topics is a must. One conversation isn't enough either. You must begin an ongoing dialogue where you and your teenager share information little by little, at their pace. This will enable him or her to grow into a person who can think competently and clearly and develop good self-control.

How can you create space for these hard conversations? Nurture and affirm your teen on a regular basis. Create a home environment where they feel safe sharing what's on their mind. Most of the time, if teens speak up, they risk retaliation, negative labeling, or worse—relentless bullying and even mental and physical harassment. Most parents aren't aware of how challenging it is for teens to publicly live out the values they have been taught.

Recently, a mom enrolled her eighth-grade son in a well-respected Christian private school, believing it would be a safe learning environment for her son. The first day of class began with kids asking some fundamental questions: "Are you new to the area?" "What school did you transfer from?" "What extracurricular activities will you try out for?" Then a classmate asked him the status of his virginity. The kids didn't even know each other! But thanks to social media, kids today don't have the same filters previous generations did. There seem to be no taboo topics among today's teens. That's why, whether the issue is sexual purity, gender-related issues, drugs and alcohol, smoking, terrorism, school violence, eating disorders, or political correctness, you can't shy away from discussing hard things with your teen.

Many parents want to believe their teens have the courage and wisdom to handle the vast societal issues they face every day. And the good news is, when provided with tools and knowledge, kids can deal with sensitive topics with confidence. Like you and me, when they understand why something matters, teens can develop strategies to say *no* and stand firm in their convictions. The list of sensitive topics we need to address is long, and at times the discussions are hard to have, but when we learn to lean into critical conversations, our relationships can deepen.

Sexual Integrity or Failure

It's hard for teens to stand firm on carefully taught biblical principles, values, and convictions in our sexually charged climate. Being bombarded by inappropriate images and explicit messages multiple times a day can wear down the sexual integrity of even the most devoted, principled teen.

We live in a world where innocent comments are quickly read as having sexual connotations. The lines of what's okay and what's not get blurry. Casual sex has become the norm, and if a teen chooses to wait until marriage before engaging in sexual activity, they get ridiculed or mocked. One thing is for sure: The pressure to compromise is great. Teens need your strength and wisdom to give them tools to remain pure under pressure. The most important tool you can arm your child with is the knowledge of what Scripture has to say about sex.

The key to helping teens navigate this area is developing a core conviction based on truth, knowledge, and understanding. When they understand why their standards matter and learn how to talk with their friends about their desire for purity, they often end up influencing others, causing them to make wise decisions for their own lives. We must teach our teens that God has much to say about waiting until marriage to become sexually intimate. Sex is a beautiful expression of love best enjoyed within the confines of marriage. Helping your teen see the value of waiting is possible as you gently yet consistently share this truth.

In our family, sexual purity is vitally important. Tom and I wanted our children to know God's standards and to experience the beauty of waiting until marriage. We were willing to do everything possible to make sure each of our kids remained pure until their wedding day. Threatening a boyfriend or locking our child inside the house wasn't the answer. Our children needed to learn principles of sexual integrity that would continue throughout their lifetime.

I've read several studies recently about students deciding to wait. I attribute that to strong parental relationships. Most teens do not have the strength to take such a stand without the influence and support of an engaged, purposeful parent. Parents reinforce their families' values on an ongoing basis. Offering gentle reminders of the importance of deciding what our kids will do ahead of time makes a difference when the temptation to give in or the pressure to go along is before them.

What can you do to help your teen with sexual integrity? Define your priorities on sexual purity, talk about them often, and give your teen a plan to accomplish these goals. For me, this meant I had to be intentional about monitoring who my kids spent time with, knowing where they were hanging out, and making sure they knew I would be checking in with them. I know this can be awkward. But although teens need freedom—more and more as they exhibit responsibility—they also need parental accountability. Unfettered freedom in this area sets them up to stumble.

The priority we place on sexual purity extends to our kids. My kids will tell you that our family talked about this topic a lot. I don't think a week passed where I wasn't talking to one of my teens about the importance of guarding their heart, being careful online, and avoiding compromising situations. I found the most effective time and place to have these conversations was at night, away from their siblings—especially since some of the siblings were of the opposite sex.

Consider the hormonal changes your teen is experiencing as well as the temptation they are under. Hormones create feelings your teen isn't used to experiencing. Feelings mixed with opportunity create irresistible desires to go a little further. When we communicate our standards—which are God's standards—teens often embrace what we teach because they trust us. Don't underestimate your influence or the power of your words. They go a long way in helping teens pursue purity.

Here are some steps to take as you talk to your teen about sexual integrity:

- Spend time as a family learning what God has to say about sexual integrity and waiting until marriage. Don't just hand your child a book and tell them to read it. That isn't enough. I once handed Jeannie a book on why we don't encourage random dating. She agreed to read it but promptly said she also wanted to read a book on why she should give dating a try. It made for some interesting conversations.

- Talk with your spouse, making sure you agree on your values and the truths you plan to share with your teen. If you aren't married, talk with a like-minded friend. Don't expect you and your spouse to share the same conviction about dating or courtship. Even if you don't completely agree, support each other in front of your teen. Discuss your differences in private.

- Explain why this topic matters to your teen. Remember, they need to know why before they follow. Teens will accept what they understand more than what they are told to do.

- Spend alone time with your teen. They will feel a measure of safety in knowing the conversation is private.

- Don't make your teen feel wrong about their feelings. It is normal to have feelings. Shaming or making them feel guilty does not create a safe environment to share those thoughts and feelings with you. Don't waste the opportunity to listen by your reaction.

- Arm your teen with truth. Your teen needs to know that not everyone is doing it. When you are diligent to teach your child the benefits of waiting, God's design for intimacy, and how to withstand the pressure they will encounter, they gain confidence to say *no* when others say *yes*.

- As much as you want what is best for your child, the decision is ultimately up to them. Even the best parenting practices won't guarantee that your teen will make the right choices. You can't make them choose to wait, but when equipped with the truth and the knowledge that they can stand firm, you can rest in knowing that they know what is right. Sexual purity is an important issue for me and one that we talked about throughout my children's teen years and into their college years. My children are all adults now. Each of them expressed gratefulness for my willingness to tell them the truth about the benefits of remaining sexually pure. Currently, three are married and two are still waiting. Though it wasn't easy, they say it was worth it. But, dear parent, if your child makes decisions you wish they didn't make, love them anyway. Show them grace. Let them know they can make better choices going forward. Don't take it personally. Chances are, it had nothing to do with you. Help them work through a bad decision in a way that helps regret turn into healing.

Gender-Related Conversations

On June 12, 2016, a man killed forty-nine people and wounded fifty-three others at Pulse, a gay nightclub in my hometown of Orlando, Florida. News of this shooting shook our city.

At the time, Tom and I hosted weekly Bible studies for high-school and college students. Shortly after the news broke, text and voice messages started pouring in from dazed and confused kids.

Many of them knew someone who was impacted by this horrible act. I was so proud of how these kids responded to the news. They were all Christians who loved the Lord. They felt the pain of loss and grief. They hurt for the hurting. We all grieved for the family members who lost loved ones and for the sons and daughters who were treating the injured. At that moment, these young people put into practice everything they had learned. Loving others. Caring for the hurting. Serving where needed.

Your beliefs on this topic need to be lovingly communicated over time and as the need arises. As parents, we share the truth, bearing in mind our goal is to keep the hearts of our teens so they will come to us seeking counsel. Teens need to learn to have compassion and love for others.

For matters related to gender and sexuality, consider the following to help get you started:

- **Seek wisdom.** Every conversation should be unique to your teen. Take some time to think about how you want to answer questions.

- **Talk often.** Teens often ask random questions. They see something or hear something and then become curious. They want to know what you think, and more importantly, why you think that way. With a sea of competing voices, yours will prevail if they know you are available to talk.

- **Pay attention.** It's easy to get sidetracked and not notice what your kid is up to. But this season of parenting needs your attention. You are shaping another life. Every conversation matters, even the ones we think they aren't listening to.

- **Ask for help.** If you aren't sure what to say or your teen asks a question about something you don't know much about, ask someone who does. Be honest and tell your teen you don't know. Then do some research and find out.

You will encounter a host of topics related to gender, transgender issues, sexual preference, and more. Teach what God has to say,[1] and help your child apply these truths in a loving way. Your teen is smart and probably knows far more than you think they know.

Drugs and Alcohol

According to the Center on Addiction, more than 90 percent of people with a substance problem started smoking, drinking, or using other drugs before their eighteenth birthday.[2] If you are like me, you're shocked that the percentage is so high. It's no secret teens partake in risky and sometimes unwise behavior—but 90 percent is concerning![3] We can help our children not become a statistic through education and engagement. Our involvement goes a long way in keeping our children safe.

Awareness of such statistics should make every parent realize what's on their teen's doorstep. Most teens will experiment with drugs and alcohol. This doesn't mean they will become addicts, but it opens a door we don't want our kids entering. While space does not allow me to address all the issues, I'll share what we did to keep drugs and alcohol at bay when the kids were teens.

- **Don't believe the lie that your kid isn't tempted.** They experience peer pressure like every other teen.

- **Invite their friends to your house to hang out.** You'd be surprised how many families don't want teenagers at their houses.

- **Create fun gatherings.** Teens enjoy a safe place to hang out with games and plenty of food. Always have food on hand.

- **Discuss what drugs and alcohol can do to them.** For some teens, knowing they are illegal or wrong only makes the desire to experience them more appealing.

Keep an eye out for symptoms of drug or alcohol usage:

- A drop in grades
- Withdrawal from the family
- Eye-drop bottles to medicate bloodshot eyes
- Change in friend groups
- Depression
- Asking for money or having issues managing money
- Getting into trouble at school or work
- Abnormal arguing or angry outbursts
- A runny or itchy nose that is not attributed to allergies or a cold
- Unusual chattiness or uncontrollable laughter for no apparent reason

With teenagers, it's not always easy to know if they are having a bad day or if they are dealing with a crisis. Being aware and willing to converse with your teen goes a long way in keeping them from experimentation.

Vaping and Smoking

You might not be familiar with vaping, but chances are, your teen is. It might surprise you to learn that at the time of this writing, "nearly 1 in 6 high school students used e-cigarettes in the past 30 days."[4] Overall, nearly 20 percent of high schoolers admit to using a tobacco product.[5] While vaping devices appear to pose fewer health risks than conventional cigarettes, they still contain harmful toxins, carcinogenic ingredients, and nicotine, a highly addictive drug.[6] Sadly, most people believe they are only getting flavor from e-cigs. Many young people are led to believe they are safe to use. The reality is, they pose health risks.[7]

The popularity of vaping in this generation is similar to the previous popularity of cigarettes. Tobacco companies have found a new product to peddle to your kid. Federal laws "prohibit companies from marketing traditional cigarettes to young people, but those laws don't apply to electronic cigarettes and other vaping devices."[8]

Parents must start talking to their children early about this topic—some say as young as five or six years old. The conversation should continue as they grow. Some glorify the habit, thinking that it is cool, so providing your child with truth equips them with information needed to say, "It's not for me."

Here are a few tips for talking to your child about smoking and vaping.

- On your way to school or a friend's house, discuss how to respond to peer pressure.

- Encourage your teen to be physically active, including being involved in sports.

- Talk about the dangers associated with smoking and vaping.

- Give them articles or research about how smoking and vaping damages lungs, can lead to cancer, and causes heart disease and shortness of breath.

- If you smoke, explain the mistake you made and how you are trying to quit.

- If you suspect your teen is smoking or hanging with friends who do, don't overreact. Ask them about it. Find out if it was a onetime event caused by curiosity or peer pressure. In either case, help them avoid addiction to this harmful habit. Your gentle, consistent guidance will help them gain the confidence to stop.

Terrorism

When our kids were growing up, we decided not to turn on the news until after the kids went to bed. If something terrible happened, I wanted to filter out what the children were exposed to and spare them the media headline. They didn't need to hear about the recent shooting or natural disaster or president's infidelity from news sources. On the morning of September 11, 2001, I was cleaning the kitchen, getting ready to start school, when Tom called to ask if I had the TV on. I quickly clicked the remote and stood in horror as I watched what was happening. Paul and Jeannie gathered around, thinking I was watching a movie, while the other kids played in another room. They were not aware that they were witnessing a real-life event. Honestly, I had a hard time processing what I saw too.

Tragedies like the World Trade Center attack devastate not only those involved but also everyone who tunes in. Today's access to breaking news through the Internet and social media has exposed our kids to unfiltered information previous generations have not had to deal with.

Here are some ways to help your teen process tragic news:

- **Pray for the people impacted by the tragedy.** My children remember how we stopped to pray for anyone involved in an auto accident as we drove by, the people harmed by the hurricanes in Houston and Florida and Puerto Rico, and even more recently, the shooting victims in Parkland, Florida. Praying for people you don't know humanizes the tragedy and encourages teens to feel empathy and compassion for their fellow citizens.

Teaching your teen to pray for others is a good way to model selflessness. Praying for others puts them in someone else's place. You'll also find that praying for others together draws you closer together.

- **Tell them the truth.** Be honest without telling every detail. Before discussing the tragedy, consider your child's age and sensitivity level. Jeannie and Paul took in information quite differently. Paul was more matter-of-fact, while Jeannie took everything to heart. She literally felt the pain others were going through. It is wise to remember that one way is not better than the other. They're just different. Respect your child's differences.

- **Shelter tweens and young teens from videos and graphic pictures.** Because tweens and younger teens are highly impacted by visual imagery, the more you can limit their exposure, the better. Older teens, while still affected by graphic images, have a greater capacity to absorb the information with less emotional turmoil.

- **Reassure your teen.** Since you can't control current events, you can and should reassure your child that you will do everything you can to protect them. If your teen feels or emotes deeply, they may fear a similar fate. Remind your kid that the Lord will always be there to guide them should something bad happen.

- **Allow your teen to mention genuine spiritual concerns.** When devastating tragedies happen, teens can be emotional and question why God allows such events. It's not unusual for them to ask thought-provoking questions. Part of learning to trust God is believing that all things happen for good (even bad things): "We know that all things work together for good to those who love God, to those who are the called according to His purpose" (Romans 8:28, NKJV). Learning takes time. Believing takes faith.

Both take practice. Remind your teen that God doesn't cause bad things to happen to us. But because of sin, we now live in a fallen world, where evil exists. If they question where God is and why he let people get hurt, be ready with truth from Scripture and remember to "preach the word; be ready in season and out of season; reprove, rebuke, and exhort, with complete patience and teaching" (2 Timothy 4:2).[9] Be understanding of their tender heart. Help them recognize that we won't always understand what good can come from an unexpected death or divorce or heartbreak. But we know God is loving and will never leave or forsake us.[10] He redeems and restores all things through the death and resurrection of Jesus. Take time to listen to the same questions over and over and over. Processing hurt and grief doesn't happen quickly. Pray with them and pray for them as they learn.

- **Give where you can.** After a tornado tore through our city, the kids and I showed up to help with the relief efforts. We didn't know what we could do, so we volunteered at Red Cross. For a couple of days, we passed out bottled water and blankets, served hot meals, and made sandwiches. It wasn't much, but my kids learned how to give of their time and aid devastated victims. This experience was one of many serving projects we did together.

School Violence

Youth violence includes a variety of behaviors. Whether it's a shooting or gang violence or a student fight, schools are not the safe zone for our kids that they once were. Some violent acts—pushing, shoving, bullying—cause damage that is more emotional than physical. A young person can be a victim, or a perpetrator, or a witness of school violence. Though not all injuries are visible, the hurt can cause anxiety, depression, and fear, which can lead to self-destructive acts—cutting, drinking, and even suicide. Your awareness of what is happening in your child's life allows you to help them cope with such issues in nonviolent ways. If you notice changes in your child's behavior, don't discount it as their just being a teenager. Dig deep to see what is causing this change. Don't assume your child will tell you what is happening, especially if they are being targeted by others. Here are some steps you can take to proactively learn what is going on with your teen:

- **Guard your mouth.** When your teen does start to talk, guard your words. If what you have to say isn't comforting or calming, then refrain from making any comments in front of your child. Not judging or overreacting keeps your teen talking.

- **Teach your teen to stay away from students who are known to cause disruptions.** Depending on the age and maturity of your teen, they might not be discerning enough to know which students to trust and which ones to avoid. They also don't fully understand the influence others have on them. There is a difference between knowing that bad company corrupts good morals and understanding how easy it is to be influenced by such company. Teens are learning how to be discerning. Your guidance will be the catalyst they need to become wise.

- **Don't rely on administrators, teachers, or coaches to know what's going on with your child.** It's normal to expect authority figures to know what is happening to your child when left in their care. Unfortunately, they rarely do. And if they do sense something is wrong, they will not address the situation in the way you would. Not because they don't care—but because they aren't you. They don't know your values, convictions, or beliefs. Use car rides, parent-teen dates, and evening chats to ask your child how things are going. Start with general questions, then move toward more specific ones. If you feel something is wrong, express interest in knowing what it is. Remind your child that you are a team. Communicate that your family does life together. Assure them that they aren't alone.

- **Teach your child how to handle a crisis.** Life is full of slipups, missteps, and plain ol' hard times. You know this, but your teen doesn't. That's why their world falls apart when a friend betrays them. As they go through the teen years, stay mindful of their lack of experience in handling a crisis.

  We live in Florida, a state known for experiencing hurricanes. Every year, we prepare for the season by discussing what we need to do before, during, and after a storm; who we need to check on (elderly parents and neighbors); and what supplies we plan to purchase. In the same way, we can prepare our children to handle crisis moments before they happen. One way you can help your teen is to role-play. No matter what the crisis is, role-playing gives them action steps to take. In any crisis, calming everyone's fears is critical. Your teen gets afraid, even if they act as if it's no big deal. Your soothing reassurance that God is in control[11] helps them feel comforted.

Changing Culture

Teens are living amid a rapidly changing culture. Some teens easily adapt while others struggle to figure out how their beliefs fit within the current culture. Everywhere they turn, their beliefs about what's right and wrong are being challenged. The freedom to speak out applies only to those who believe what our "tolerant" society considers acceptable—and what is acceptable changes frequently. Teaching your child to hold on to their core convictions without becoming a target takes wisdom. But no matter how powerful cultural influence seems, you can teach your kid that they don't have to conform to cultural standards that aren't rooted in a biblical worldview.

Helping your teen navigate such cultural changes is a worthy investment of your time. Here's the list I created before talking to my kids about how to stand firm in a culture that wants them to just agree:

- Pray first.
- Give them freedom to ask or disagree.
- Talk about guarding their heart.
- Show them why they need to be diligent.
- Talk about forming a biblical strategy to answer others' questions.
- Talk about the need for a support system.
- Talk about your family values.
- Remind them whose they are: They belong to God first and your family second.
- Paint a visual picture of living a life pleasing to the Lord.

Teens must be equipped to stand up for what they believe. Their confidence to do so emerges from knowing the truth. Once they understand the truth, they can defend their position in a healthy and wise way. God does not want us to hide or be afraid to speak up, but if we learn to show love to those with whom we don't agree, we leave the door open for future conversation. Most teens who came to our home over the years wanted to know how to discuss cultural issues in a way that wasn't confrontational. They asked deep questions about what others believed and why it mattered. This generation is eager to make a difference. They want to be taught and come to their own conclusions. If you aren't willing to teach them, then someone else will. Please let it be you!

FEELING RESPONSIBLE

It's hard when a child chooses to behave in reckless or destructive ways, but when you feel personally responsible, it's even harder. For many years, I took most of my teens' poor decisions personally. If only I had done this or said that or explained a little more, then they would have made better choices! They wouldn't have been in that place at that time! They wouldn't have sought out that negative influence for a friend! I know many of you struggle with these thoughts as well. It's normal to feel this way.

Or you might be on the front end of your parenting-a-teen journey. You've watched what others have done, and you're determined to get it right. You aren't going to neglect your responsibilities or set a poor example. You're going to be committed to your faith and feel confident that your teen will escape the common pitfalls of growing up. But whether you've been faithful to your parenting vision for a while or are just now determining to tackle sensitive topics head-on, you must cling to this truth: Your child's decisions are their decisions.

All of my kids were taught the same values, and each of them had to make and then take responsibility for their decisions. As parents, we can do everything we know to do to help our teens navigate this season well and still have to walk through some significant challenges. The reality is that we are all broken. No matter our parenting choices, some kids don't follow what they've been taught. They want to do life their way, on their terms.

Your teen's decisions will become part of their story—for better or worse. The enemy will use their decisions to cause chaos within your family. Your teen might accuse you of not parenting well. That's what some teens do—they blame others. But their decisions are not your shame or guilt to own. You are parenting them to the best of your ability before the Lord, and you need to understand where your responsibility ends and theirs begins.

Of course, you will struggle with questions, with shame and guilt over the decisions your teen makes. But God doesn't expect you to carry those emotions. Take them to the Lord. Consider the following as you wrestle with your child's choices:

- Ask the Lord to search your heart as you examine your parenting practices. Allow him to reveal areas where you can change your parenting. Remember, you are learning to parent the child God gave you.

- Parenting—even Christian parenting—is not easy. We are not guaranteed our children will do everything right. A child who participates in risky or promiscuous behavior reminds us of our need for the Lord. Don't forget that many well-respected parents have had wayward children.

- Holding on to guilt or shame only keeps you from loving your son or daughter unconditionally. I know how hard it is to let go of mistakes. But to be the parent, you must.

- It is always too soon to quit. Your struggling teen needs unconditional love now more than ever. It can be challenging to know when to pull back and when to pursue. Don't let your hurt or heartbreak trap you from moving the relationship forward.

- Separate what your teen does from who they are. These are different things. Who we are at the core is not always reflective of what we do.

- You aren't in control. That position belongs to the Lord. He alone knows the heart and mind of your child. He has a plan for that precious life. He will use every mishap and mistake.

- You don't know the end of the story. This is only a chapter in their life. Chances are, your teen will look back on this season and tell your grandkids about how you helped them get through a difficult time.

The best decision you can make when your child gets derailed is to help them learn to own their decisions. Learning to accept poor choices and turn their behavior around is a skill they will use throughout their life. If your daughter admits to cutting or having an eating disorder, she will be more receptive to hearing the counsel of others. If your son confesses to lying about his online activity, he is more willing to agree with the screen-access restrictions you place on him. As my husband, Tom, says, "Put the ball in their court." Allow them the dignity of taking responsibility for and dealing with their own problems. Be willing to help them, realizing you will have to bear more of the burden until they get stronger. You will have to judge when to step in and seek outside help. You may have to assess their capacity to deal with the situation they're in. If your teen is unwilling to listen to you, refuses to obey your instructions, or starts to blame you for their poor choices, you might have a long road to recovery and restoration. Don't lose hope. God isn't finished with your teen, or you. As long as you continue to show them love despite what they do, rebuilding the relationship bridge is possible.

As you face the fallout of your child's decisions, be aware of the impact on your marriage. You and your spouse might not agree on how to address the issues before you. It's not easy when two parents disagree on how to handle their child, but be honest with each other about how your child's predicament is affecting you, your spouse, and your child's siblings. As parents support each other, the kids gain a broader perspective on how to respond in the family context. For example, the dad needs to establish what is unacceptable behavior toward his wife. This one small act on Tom's part changed how my teenage boys spoke to me. Suddenly I wasn't just their mother—I was their dad's wife.

The best gift you can give your child is to maintain a healthy marriage. Build safeguards to ensure your relationship will be intact once they leave home.

Walking through teen struggles is infinitely harder without a support system. Sometimes it becomes necessary to seek help outside your family. Don't be afraid to approach trusted friends for prayer support, empathy, guidance, or help. And, depending on the severity of the situation, your family might benefit from counseling. During this time, pray. Pray that your responses will be life-giving. Pray for your teen's heart to be bent toward the Lord and you. Guard against resentment toward your child for their actions. And don't give up on the vision of having a strong, healthy relationship with your teen.

MISHAPS AND MISTAKES

Making mistakes and breaking the rules is normal behavior. I would love to tell you otherwise, but it's what teens do. Whether they obey everything we say or not isn't the point. Our response is. Our job is to set expectations and rules and administer consequences when they don't meet those expectations or follow the rules. Our role is to advise and guide them.

When they make crash landings, our kids need to know one thing above all else: that we still love them. We might feel responsible or angry or resentful or hurt, but we need to take those struggles to the Lord. When we run to the one who made our children, then we are free to love them the way God loves us.

Consider these words of Paul: "I am sure of this, that he who began a good work in you will bring it to completion at the day of Jesus Christ" (Philippians 1:6). And Philippians 4:6 reminds us, "In everything by prayer and supplication with thanksgiving let your requests be made known to God." Our kids will make mistakes; we will make mistakes. When mistakes and mishaps happen, we can trust that God will use them for good.

We all have hopes and expectations about what our children will become. But we often confuse our role by believing we should plan their lives instead of simply dreaming with them about what they will do. The real goal should be to equip them to be the people

God created them to be and prepare them for adult life. They will feel competent in this when they have skills and talents developed through trying and failing, trying again—and succeeding.

When you talk about sensitive topics, stress the importance of integrity. Teach your child a simple concept they can hold on to when faced with difficult decisions: *Don't do anything today that you will have to lie about tomorrow.* The decisions your teen makes every day shape and define their integrity. Reminding them of this fact may make you unpopular for the moment. However, you aren't raising a teen for the moment; you are investing in their future.

You are the most influential person in your teen's life. Take advantage of that role! Keep your relationship healthy and the lines of communication open so they feel comfortable coming to you with sensitive topics. It is worth the investment of time and energy.

WRAPPING IT UP

- What do you need to adjust in your attitude and approach in order to ask questions in a gentle manner that doesn't communicate that you're trying to argue? How can you encourage your child to be intentional about becoming the person God uniquely created them to be?

- Do you talk frequently about sexual purity? If not, pick a time and place where you can bring up the conversation and start equipping your teen to pursue purity and wait for sex until marriage.

- If your child has made an unwise decision, how did you respond? How do you wish you had responded? How can you take intentional steps to respond differently in the future?

- Are you afraid to bring up hard-to-discuss questions? How can you push through that fear so that if your teen wants to talk with someone, you will be that someone?

- How can you and your spouse get on the same page regarding sensitive topics you need to discuss with your teen? Make a list and set a time to share your thoughts. Be intentional about hearing your spouse's point of view. Find common areas of agreement and focus on those as you engage with your teen.

Chapter 10

SQUASH YOUR FEAR

I SO WANT TO BE A GOOD PARENT. I desire for my children to look back on their childhoods with great memories. I know perfect parents don't exist, but during my kids' growing-up years, I feared I was doing it all wrong. After all, I didn't have a strong foundation when I began my parenting journey.

Although there are no perfect parents or perfect children, it is possible to be the parent God called you to be. He says, "Fear not, for I am with you" (Isaiah 41:10). Those words got me through some difficult parenting years, and they will get you through too. Knowing that God has equipped you with everything you need to parent will provide security as you raise your child.

Fear can wreak havoc in our homes if not dealt with properly. Parents, if you're not careful, you can fall into the trap of fearing that your actions will result in your teen's rebelling against you. You must remember that you can't effectively parent from a place of fear.

Instead, establish and maintain confidence in knowing God is with you and will lead you. Your teen is God's child. He has a plan for them. While your teen might not always agree with you or your position, the fear factor cannot paralyze you and keep you from doing what is best for your relationship. You must remember that perfect love casts out all fear (see 1 John 4:18).

To avoid letting fear rule your parenting style, separate the problem from the child. Many times, when we get upset or angry, we take the words and actions of our teens personally—and respond poorly. I found that I'd speak to someone else (such as a boss or a friend) more carefully than I'd speak to my child. As your parenting changes and you start thinking of your teen as a young adult, you will naturally change how you speak to them.

Remember that your teen sees the situation through their filters. Your child didn't grow up in your childhood. You are creating a new legacy with different childhood memories. Don't bring your fears and unresolved issues from the past into the future. Your child should not have to relive your childhood. Changing your mind-set allows you to focus on two main points: the situation and the relationship. Objectively and accurately assess any given situation and react accordingly. Remember, it's not about who's right. It's about establishing and securing a close relationship with your child. What will be gained if someone is always right but ends up not having the respect of the family?

FEAR OF REJECTION

The fear of rejection is powerful—so powerful, in fact, that it's one of the primary reasons parents are fearful. Will their children reject them? The truth is, no one wants to experience rejection. We want to be accepted and adored by those we love most. So a fear of rejection can manifest itself through constant worry that your child won't love you or fear that your child won't accept your leadership. We parents basically fear that our children will end up resenting the choices we made concerning them and point out everything we did wrong. We shouldn't parent from a place of fear, but of faith. When you are committed to working together, fear has no place to live.

At times throughout the teenage years, your child will reject what you say. You can't take that personally because it's not necessarily a rejection of you. You have to look at children as people first—people who have their own ideas. Look at them as they're trying to sort it all out, and be consistent. Be persistent and unwavering in your confidence that you are leading them in the right way and doing what is best for them. If something is not working, however, have the confidence to make a course correction. Many times during our parenting journey, we needed to make changes. It was natural as the family grew and we saw more clearly and understood situations differently. It is okay to change.

Sometimes we carry old baggage and issues from our own childhoods into our new families. Maybe your parents never approved of or affirmed you. Maybe your parents let you get away with everything or didn't let you get away with anything. We can approach our parenting with the mind-set of "My parents were like this, so I'm not going to be like that" and "My parents didn't do this, so I'm going to do this." That's not the right approach to parenting. You should define or refine your parenting style by knowing the truth contained in God's Word. Your child is a gift. They are wonderfully made (see Psalm 139:14), and their life has meaning. The principles you teach them will become their road map. Believe this truth. Learn more about it. Take it to heart, and place it at the core of everything you do as a parent.

Teaching and training your child in the way they should go doesn't mean they are going to accept your guidance every step of the way. It means you are going to impart truths to them every day, teaching them a little here and there. That's a critical mind-set for getting through the teen years—knowing that it's not going to be accomplished in a day. Your child isn't going to praise you every morning. You don't have to worry that you've ruined them for life if you say something wrong or don't do something for them every time they need it. Always remember the redemptive value of these very powerful words: "I'm sorry; please forgive me."

That doesn't negate the fact that whether you're afraid of your child's rejection or not, you've got to teach them the way they should go (see Proverbs 22:6). Teaching them truths and principles is your assignment. Not in the way *you* think they should go, but in the way *they should go*. They are a mirror of you. They are a mirror of their Creator. And those principles don't change. You are equipping them for the life they were created to live.

In dealing with fear, remember 1 John 4:18: "Perfect love casts out fear." Every time you feel fearful, give those thoughts and feelings to the Lord. Lay down your anxiety, anger, impatience, worry, doubt, and frustration. When you starve your fears, your faith will grow.[1] Then you will be free to trust God as you seek to keep the heart of your teen. Remember, too, that your child is God's child, and you are a steward commanded to carry out a job for him. Knowing that God is the architect, consult him on his plan for your child.

As you look around, you'll see someone who seems to have an easier time of it or looks as if she has it all together, but you don't know what's happening on the inside. We do our families a disservice when we compare ourselves to others. You are parenting in your family according to the way God is leading you!

Moms frequently say that conflict with their teens starts as a non-verbal exchange—the children roll their eyes or don't answer them respectfully. The mom of a fourteen-year-old young man once shared how her son told her, "Mom, you never let us have anything or do anything. But if I go and ask Dad, he will get it." In that moment, she feared her son had completely rejected her. Many of us feel our kids won't love us if we don't give them what they're asking for at that moment. Stop and tell yourself the truth. You aren't parenting for their happiness or instant gratification. God has given you a much higher calling.

Deep within the heart of a mother is a gripping thought that her teen will grow up and either not love her or think that she's a terrible mother. I know I felt that way, and many of my friends did too. If we are not careful, that fear can drive us to make unwise decisions. It can also cause us to become more frustrated with our children, which makes them even unhappier with us. Now we've placed ourselves in a vicious cycle: We desperately try to be loved and appreciated for all we do, but we're driving our children away from us.

FEAR OF REBELLION

The word *rebellion* seems synonymous with *teenagers*. There are two forms of rebellion: rebellion that is overtly defiant, and rebellion that emerges from a desire for independence. Knowing the difference can save you countless arguments. We picture yelling, stubbornness, disrespect, and teens' not doing what they are told as rebellious acts against authority. But what if such behaviors are nothing more than an immature child's desire to become an independent person? The fear of rebellion—a deep-seated worry that your child will run toward something or get caught up in something that is not good for them—is legitimate. They might get caught up with the wrong set of friends or begin unacceptable relationships. They may start struggling internally. Even in those situations, you cannot let fear of *what if* take hold of you. Take time to pause, pray, and reflect on what you need to do to help them through their struggles and keep their heart in the process. Talk with close friends who can support you. Look for ways you can adjust your requests or expectations to allow your teen more flexibility. You want them to learn how to resolve differences, and they do this by remembering that their life has meaning, they belong to your family, and they are an overcomer.

FEAR OF PARENTAL PEER PRESSURE

Another issue that causes fear is parental peer pressure. Parents don't think about this much, but they're faced with just as much peer pressure as kids are. Think about the ripple effect that occurs in your circle of friends when one parent buys her child a new car or lets her child go to the beach with five friends—things you don't do. Your best friend may host a lavish birthday party or allow her kids to play mature video games or watch TV shows that you don't think are appropriate.

As the parent, you need to guard against the same peer pressure that you've warned your kid about. Stay firm in your decisions. Keep a united front with your spouse. Move forward without fear, regardless of whether your friends approve of your parenting style or decisions.

Fear can also stem from worry that if you don't do what your friends are doing, you might not stay friends. That's okay—you might not. You might have friends that journey with you only a short time, but you can't compromise your parenting convictions and your love for and relationship with your child just so you can retain a certain segment of friends.

There have been times we've lost friends because we didn't dress our kids a certain way or follow a specific parenting program. Our friends strongly believed that what they were doing was right, so they judged what we were doing as wrong. We just held to our convictions and loved them enough to let them go on their way while we went on our way. Our conviction was to follow our faith and do the best we knew how, daily learning and growing. We weren't raising their kids; we were raising ours. When we see these couples, we wave, smile, and are friendly, but our families can't enjoy a relationship together because unconditional acceptance is missing.

FEAR OF CONFLICT

Most parents want to avoid conflict. Sometimes it's not possible. If you discover your teen is manipulating you or lying to make you look bad, you must deal with the situation. Turning a blind eye will not make the issue go away. You must take a step back and look at the situation not as something you win in order to show your ultimate control and authority but as a situation where you can work with your teen toward a resolution.

Parents also fear that their kids won't accurately portray what's really happening in the home. They are afraid their children will say something to an authority figure that would make the parents look bad. You cannot parent out of fear of what your child might or might not say. As long as you are doing the right thing and not breaking any laws, then you can't worry about what your child might say. However, you want to have sound wisdom, guard your mouth, choose your words carefully, and always remember to focus on the relationship.

God clearly says that parents are responsible for their children.[2] That's it. The school system, principal, grandparents, and friends— they aren't responsible for your teen in the eyes of the Lord. You are! As parents, we will give an answer to the Lord for how we raised our children. God gave you your child, and he gave them to you to teach and to train for his glory to the best of your ability. He doesn't want us to be gripped with fear. We need to starve the fear and rest in knowing God is at work. Choosing to focus on this truth will help you combat the fear of what others may think.

Being strong and confident in the way you're going and the way you're leading the family, and being consistent in that path, ultimately helps your child realize you're doing this for their good, not for yours. So when the conflict is over, take time to remind your child (not in a retaliatory way or with an angry or frustrated tone) that your desire is for their good. Your desire is for them to do well.

At the conclusion of any conflict, teach them how to restore harmony. Don't skip over this important step in haste. Through the emotional act of coming together, the relationship is made stronger. They trust that you're going to be available for them unconditionally as they struggle and try to find their way. They gain security in knowing that you love them—that no one loves them more than you.

Avoid falling into the trap of being fearful during conflict. Challenges and problems don't have to result in your teen's resenting you. You must remember that you can't parent from a place of fear. Rather, enter hard conversations with confidence, knowing God is with you and will lead you.

FEAR OF EMBARRASSMENT

Most of us want our teens to be shining examples for all to see. We post picture after picture of proud-mom moments: our teens winning awards, serving others, doing well in school. Some might think we are just bragging, but the truth is, parents are delighted when their children do something good. These are moments that give us hope that we are doing a good job.

While we don't like to talk openly about it, parents often operate out of fear of the opposite kind of moments. We are afraid our teenagers might do something that will reflect poorly on them—or on us. But this is a dangerous trap to fall into. Our children's worth is not based on performance or on the approval of others. Ultimately, we want our kids to desire to do things that please the Lord and to not do things that do not honor him. It is wiser to focus on our children and not on what someone might think of our families.

Your teen will probably do things that will embarrass you. Like you, they are imperfect and, at times, self-centered. When they make poor choices, we have an opportunity to respond in a way that will serve them and our relationships well. Not all decisions come from the same motivation; it's important to consider who your child is and why they're acting in this way. Reflect on the behavior and determine what your child is trying to say. Is it merely an expression of who she is, or is it an expression of her dislike of the pressures society places on her? Understanding where the behavior is coming from can help you determine the best approach to resolving the situation.

- **Misguided independence.** Teens have a strong desire to break away and be their own bosses. Unfortunately, their attempts to do so often get them in trouble. They decide to go to a movie instead of hanging out at a friend's house. They eat the food you needed for making dinner that night. They start telling you what they are doing instead of asking if they can. Or maybe they do something more serious, like slip out after you've gone to bed to meet up with some friends. Maybe you've woken up to the sound of your phone ringing at 1:30 a.m., and your child—the one who is supposed to be in bed—is on the other end, crying hysterically because they've been in a fender bender.

  Without much thought, teenagers do careless and even foolish things in their effort to express themselves as individuals. After everyone has had time to gather their thoughts, you need to have deliberate conversations about acceptable behavior and the consequences for their actions. No need to try to correct them in the moment when you're stressed or angry. Start your conversation with asking *why* questions. When teenagers have a healthy sense of family identity, the desire to please and honor their parents becomes a motivating factor to avoid behavior that would displease them. They make this choice not out of fear but out of love. Your firm but gentle rebuke reminds them of how your family lives.

- **Disagreement.** When more than one person lives in the same house, disagreements will happen. No matter how good a parent you are, sometimes your teen will suddenly decide they don't want to do what you would like for them to do. They don't agree with your principles; they don't agree with you. As much as this breaks your heart, you get to decide how to respond. You are the adult. Are you going to cut them off relationally or financially to get them to comply? Or are you going to take time to discover the reason why they disagree? If they don't like your rules or believe your values or agree with how you clean the kitchen—or any number of things—keep calm. Yes, it is your house. Yes, you can make them do what you say. But there is another way. You need to parent beyond your rules if you want to keep the heart of your child. Whatever you do, don't get into the game of "Who's going to win?" That's not the goal of raising children. Turning a situation into a win-or-lose battle will cause wounds on all sides until all you're left with is an empty relationship. Either everyone wins in a relationship or everyone loses.

- **Poor choices.** You may encounter times when your child doesn't mean to embarrass you but has made a decision that significantly affects the family. How you respond can cultivate your relationship and encourage your child toward long-term wholeness or shut them down. For example, a woman I'll call Kathy got pregnant in high school and decided to give the baby up for adoption. In the face of embarrassment and the life-changing choice their daughter made, Kathy's parents responded with wisdom and grace. Not long after the baby was born, they attended church with their daughter, the baby, and the baby's new adoptive parents. Their love and support of their child through such an emotional time made a powerful impact on their relationship and those around them.

In contrast, another woman I know received no support at all from her parents when she got pregnant. They forced her to give the baby up for adoption and focused more on their embarrassment than on their relationship with their daughter. Decades later, the daughter still does not have a close relationship with her parents. Living and responding out of grace—even if our children make mistakes or do things we don't agree with—is a crucial way to protect our relationships with our children.

Be prepared with how you will respond before problematic actions ever take place, and you'll be prepared to respond in a healthy and constructive way. Memorizing these six steps will help you keep things calm as you work through the issue.

- Don't overreact.
- Separate the act from the child.
- Don't take offense.
- Maintain self-control. This applies to you *and* your teen!
- Don't shame them publicly.
- Remember that they are learning.

A teen once told me that her parents did not want her to pierce her nose. She thought about it, then decided her parents were being too restrictive. When she went to the mall with a group of her friends, she saw a jewelry store that advertised free piercings with the purchase of gold studs. Her friends encouraged her to get it done.

Put yourself in these parents' shoes. What if your child came home one day having ignored a boundary you set? How you react will either cultivate a closer relationship or put a wedge between your teen and yourself. This isn't about whether piercings are right or wrong—this kind of situation goes beyond the action itself. As parents, we need to carefully consider our responses because our reactions will hinder or help our relationships. The relationship is more important than what your teen does or how they perform.

Successful parenting is not about what other people think. It's about nurturing, fostering, guarding, and protecting your relationship with your teen. As you choose not to base your response on fear of embarrassment, you will cultivate a relationship that allows you to speak God's truth to your teen in a way they will hear. It's your job to point your child to the Lord. The stronger your relationship is, the more your child will listen to what you have to say. You are the primary influence in their life. However, you are not their final authority. Their Creator is.

FEAR AND TRUST

I've spoken to many parents who are afraid. There is one justifiable fear: that we as parents will not faithfully raise the children he gave us well. It's true that God says, "To whom much [is] given, of him much [is] required" (Luke 12:48). God has given us humans to teach and train. This is our primary job as parents. Much is required of us in how we guide and direct our children toward the Lord. We are to be humble (see James 4:10), not easily angered (see Proverbs 14:29), full of grace and understanding (see Psalm 49:3), and slow to speak and quick to hear (see James 1:19). We can be all these and more. But we must ask the Lord to replace our fear with confidence by helping us trust him to provide all we need to do the job. Then we can rest knowing how to starve the fear of parenting teenagers.

At the end of your journey, God will ask you, "What did you do with the child I gave you? Did you nurture them, did you point them toward me, did you care for them, and did you train them up in the way they should go?" There were many times when my teenagers and I would not see eye to eye about something, and it wasn't always a right-or-wrong issue. It was just a preference or a hunch that something was not quite right. When this happened, I would look at them and say, "You know I have to stand before the Lord and answer for every word I say, every action I take, and the way I lead you. And I want to be found faithful on that day." I'm confident you want to be faithful to teach them well too.

Your teenager learns to trust the Lord as they see you seek and follow him. He is the architect, and he knows exactly why he gave that child to you. He equips you to do all that he asks.

The teenage years can be a delightful, joyous time, as long as you ignore the fears that enter your mind. Fear is not from the Lord. Fear is from the enemy. Parent from a place of confidence in who God is, knowing that this is his child, given to you as a gift to raise for his glory and his Kingdom so that they may live out his plan for them.

WRAPPING IT UP

- What are your greatest fears about raising a teenager?

- Are you afraid of looking bad to others because of your parenting decisions or the choices your teenager makes? Where does that fear come from?

- How do you want to handle embarrassing situations? Write down your thoughts, and discuss them with your spouse.

- List three things that cause you fear, and identify how you can overcome those fears.

Chapter 11

STAY ENGAGED

WHAT DOES A TEEN NEED? As my first child entered the teen years, I found myself asking this critical question every day. For decades, parents have wrestled with what to do—and what *not* to do—when raising teens. Do teens need to be challenged or coddled—or a combination of both? I encourage you to consider these questions instead: *What do they need you to be, and what do they need from you?*

Most teens can't identify or express what they need. But as parents, we must recognize that they need much more from us than food, money, and the keys to the car. Children of every age need their parents to be the strong, sturdy shade trees that supply nutrients to the branches and leaves.

Even though our teenagers are moving toward adulthood, they still need help. The fast-paced world teens are growing up in, coupled with their personal physical changes, can be overwhelming. But our encouragement will get them through. That is why it's vital to remember they still need us, even when they don't say it. In many ways, they need us now more than ever.

WHAT YOUR TEEN NEEDS

Until now, you've known how to be the parent your child needs. Protect them from danger. Be responsible. Be available, or try to be. Stay aware. And you've upheld your end of the deal. Chances are, you've done a good job of parenting! But with every passing day, your confidence gets shaken and your joy turns to frustration. One morning, your teen adopts an attitude as they head off to school. You question whether you did something wrong. Then you assume they must just be having a bad day. A few days later, they "forget" to say good-bye or give you a hug when they dash out the door for practice. Then they start grunting instead of saying good morning (as they've done since preschool). What is going on? You scratch your head and wonder what your teen needs from you now.

Keep in mind that adolescence is just a phase. Your child's basic need for protection, responsibility, availability, and awareness from you remains the same. But the *way* they need you changes. Yes, change often comes suddenly and without notice. I remember being caught off guard when some of my kids stopped coming up to me after a game to give me a hug. I experienced a range of emotions: hurt, anger, resentment, and frustration. But I realized that each child needed me differently than they used to.

Protection

We've spent a lot of time talking about what it takes to build a strong relationship with your teen as you prepare them for adulthood: easing up on rules and letting them apply the principles they've learned. And yes, to parent well in this season, you must—and must continue to—provide freedom and space for your child so that they make healthy transitions from childhood to adulthood. But I would be remiss if I didn't reiterate the importance of providing protection and guidance during this critical season. Teens still need protecting. A wise parent doesn't turn her child loose to do as he or she pleases. Good parents provide healthy protection for their children, not to keep them from failing or trying but to keep them from unforeseen harm. We do this by being aware of our children's peer groups and of hidden dangers our children may face.

PEER GROUPS

Teens are easily influenced by what they hear and see, especially from their peers. This is evident by the way they stress over clothes, friends, and music. They are too young to realize they are being influenced, yet they are old enough to understand how much friends matter.

Why do we need to protect our children from the wrong peer groups? Because those teenagers influence our kids. Honestly, we are all influenced to some degree by what our friends do or say. If we aren't careful, our teens could end up following others instead of doing what they know is right.

We are warned of this in 1 Corinthians 15:33. The apostle Paul wrote, "Bad company corrupts good morals" (NASB). I'll never forget the morning my son Paul called us to ask if we knew where his car was. What an odd question! It was supposed to be in the driveway. He then told us that the police were at our front door. They had found his car in an orange grove, stripped of all electronics and burned to a crisp. Once we recovered from our shock, we asked for more details. The officer said it appeared to be part of a gang initiation. Kids will do daring, even illegal, acts if it means gaining acceptance to something or from someone. The opposite is also true. Teens can be persuaded to commit acts of kindness due to the influence of those around them. Peer groups influence teens either for good or for bad. Your discernment and willingness to be engaged play a vital part in helping your teen avoid peers who won't bring out their best.

HIDDEN DANGERS

As a parent, you are well aware of the dangers capable of hurting your child, causing division, and destroying relationships. These dangers will vary based on the child and the situation, so it can be helpful to have a larger perspective of your role, no matter what you and your teen encounter.

At the beginning of this chapter, I mentioned the idea that your child needs you to be like a big, strong, healthy shade tree. This kind of tree—full of leaves, with healthy branches, a sturdy trunk, and deep roots—is able to withstand the fiercest storms. When my kids were younger, I explained our role as parents in this way:

> Dad and I provide shelter and protection from the storms of life and from everything you need protection against, including the things you can't see, issues you are unaware of, and dangers that can harm you. We are the tree.
>
> Each part of the tree serves a purpose. The leaves provide a reprieve from the hot sun and offer shelter during an afternoon shower. The branches are for those who need rest from flying, providing a safe place to rest until they are ready to take flight again. The trunk supports the branches and leaves. If the trunk is weak, the tree will be blown around in a storm and won't provide reliable protection for those in need. The roots are the true strength of the tree. If the root system is not deep, the tree will fall during the mildest storm. The roots also provide nourishment to keep the entire tree healthy.

This example has several useful takeaways as we consider how to protect our kids from the various hidden dangers they'll encounter.

First, we need to take care of ourselves as individuals. Second, we must take care of our relationships as couples. Third, we must focus on teaching our children when to venture out and when to rest.

If you neglect taking care of yourself, you get weak. When you get too busy with life to take care of each other, you both get weak. When you are weak, you aren't alert to what your child needs; thus, they become weak. Once your child understands how you offer protection, you can explain how they will benefit from this protection if they are willing to.

A wise person knows when to seek shelter and when to venture out; a foolish person acknowledges the value of a tree but refuses to take refuge under it. In the same way, parents give freedom to do certain things, but with this freedom, the child is required to show responsibility and discernment. Their wisdom is measured by the choices they make. You can't protect them if they aren't wise enough to seek your help.

As your teen becomes older and more mature, they should venture out. This is when they put into action everything you've equipped them with. They are ready! Should situations become unmanageable, however, they know you are there for them.

You must find the delicate—and crucial—balance between letting your child take risks and protecting them from harm. Help your child understand that you not are trying to keep them from venturing out—you are trying to protect them from dangerous situations they might not be ready to handle. They may feel you are overprotective, but how you communicate your thoughts can reveal your good intentions. As you reinforce this by your actions, they come to learn that this isn't about you adding restrictions but about expressing your love for them.

As teens get older, protecting them from hurt, harm, and destruction becomes more challenging. They believe they are smart and capable enough. Some think they are invincible. They won't be able to avoid every hidden danger, and you won't be able to keep them from those things. But if your child knows you are there for them, even if they stumble, you are filling one of their greatest needs—protection—during this season of life.

Responsibility

Your teen is learning about responsibility from you. How do you handle the responsibilities in your life, particularly concerning the needs of those around you? The phrase *more is caught than taught* is fitting when it comes to the area of responsibility. Your teen needs to see you living a responsible life, not just hear you talk about doing so.

Your responsibilities change according to the age and personality of your kid; some kids tend to be more independent, while others need you for an extended time. It's paramount to your future relationship with your child that you identify their individual needs and modify your behavior or your busyness to address those needs. Independent children get comfortable with your absence if you are too busy, and they sometimes develop a passiveness, allowing them to become detached from you. While they don't think they need as much attention from you, they still do. Some kids understand this sooner because you have fostered such a transparent and open relationship with them.

Your kid also watches how you handle difficult responsibilities, such as taking care of your own parents and the occasional crisis that might arise. They learn from how you manage these issues, whether you bemoan helping other people or joyfully look for ways to serve somebody in need. If you do the latter, you are modeling outward thinking instead of self-centeredness to your kid, helping them to understand all the things you do for them and for others. However, if your kid sees you doing a lot for others while neglecting your own family, seeds of resentment can build up, eroding the very relationship and trust you are trying to foster. If you are unavailable, they learn that they are not a priority to you. It's important to find the proper balance between caring for yourself and being responsible for your child, however hard that may be.

If we don't focus on taking proper care of who we are, we can become emotionally drained or too weary. Our teens won't be as emotionally, mentally, or physically strong, either. As connections start to dry out or priorities change due to our lack of self-care, the relationship begins to weaken.

As a parent, you also have a responsibility to teach your child how to tend to their own life. They need you to help them make wise decisions regarding proper nutrition, exercise, and sleep. How do you do this? Through modeling good choices in your own life.

You know the drill: You stay up till 3:00 a.m. working on an art project or sewing the last costume for the play, knowing you have to get up at 6:00 a.m. to get the kids up and ready for their day. With eyes half-closed, you grab a couple of cups of coffee, but they aren't enough. You seem to drag all day, and by the time evening rolls around, you are ready to send the kids to bed. You are exhausted. And then you hear, "Mom, I need help with this homework that's due tomorrow."

Frustrated at your child's lack of planning, you get snippy at her; she gets snarky with you. Your lack of sleep makes it hard to hide your frustration. You look up with pursed lips and a scowl on your face. She clearly interprets your thoughts. You ask her why she waited so late, reminding her she needs to be more responsible. You agree to help because you don't want her to fail. But you grumble the entire time. She feels your disapproval. The evening of rest you wanted so badly has turned into an evening of stress. When you finally crawl into bed, you realize you are overscheduled, and you both paid the price tonight.

If you're trying to teach your child the value of sleep but you don't model this practice, your teen will notice and question why it doesn't apply to you. Sleep is important. Brain development requires sleep for brain circuitry to function properly. If you treat sleep—or any other values you have for your teen—as important, your teen is more likely to do so as well. Lead by example.

Besides being responsible for yourself and for modeling wise choices, you are responsible for your teen's actions. If your son breaks a neighbor's window, it's your responsibility to make sure it is replaced. Likewise, when your child gets her license and starts to drive, her safety—and the safety of other drivers she meets on the road—is your responsibility.

Your teen needs you to be a reliable parent who lives responsibly. They also need to know that their actions and misdeeds can negatively impact their parents. Parents are responsible for their teens' actions and will be held accountable for what they do and how they behave should something happen to others. The idea that they can call the shots with no recourse, or that Mom and Dad will bail them out every time they do something, is unacceptable. They need you to show them what a responsible life looks like, but they also need to know that they share in the responsibility too.

Mutual responsibility is the basis for how your family will function. Wise children will not grieve or bring shame to their parents. Instead, they will listen to their parents' instructions and consider the impact of their actions. Will they slip up or choose to ignore any of these? Maybe. But don't feel like a failure when they act irresponsibly. Get up, dust everyone off, and start again (and again).

Availability

Teens don't want to be lectured. Lectures didn't work when your parents used them; they don't work when you use them, either. But your teen does need you to be available to talk. They need you to understand the best ways to engage with them and communicate what they need to hear.

- **Be just what they need.** Teens only want information they need *right now*. Remember, teens learn on a need-to-know basis. They need you to explain why they should listen before you jump right into what you think they need to hear.

- **Don't be predictable.** Find a fresh way to make your point. Be creative.

- **Understand their shorter attention span.** You have only a few seconds to grab their attention. Once they know why they need to listen, get to the content, and be ready to listen to their responses.

- **Be direct.** Don't take too much time to get to the point. They will pay more attention and appreciate you for not wasting time.

- **Help them learn to balance.** They can easily overcommit and find themselves running on fumes. Teaching balance means helping them learn their limits.

- **Don't be afraid to do things differently.** Your friends might be parenting differently than you. That's okay. Teach your teen that every family is different. Your teen will appreciate your willingness to set high expectations for your family.

- **Use word pictures.** Today's teens are highly image driven. Use effective metaphors to illustrate your point. Use a story format, and keep it on point.

- **Make your point stick.** They don't have time to remember every detail. Add relevant twists. Teens like suspense. They've heard your lectures for years. They know how the conversation is going to go. Surprise them.

- **Focus on one point.** If you want them to remember your point, focus on one theme. Don't let yourself ramble.

Awareness

Your teen is listening, watching, and learning from you. They need you to help guide them in the things they are facing. This takes awareness of what they need to hear or learn at any given time and in any given situation. They need you to help them

- **Understand the meaning of life.** Teens have a need to feel the work they do is making a difference. Studies reveal today's teens are more interested in making a difference than in making a lot of money. They want to enjoy life and work. Gone are the days of people working forty hours a week for thirty years, then retiring to finally do something they want to do. Teens want to do what they enjoy *now*.

- **Learn to focus.** Teens are bombarded with new ideas, causes, and activities every day. They believe they can solve world hunger, stop child abuse, and change the world. The only problem is that they don't know where to begin. Helping them map out a plan and develop action items keeps them turning to you for guidance and prevents them from getting exhausted.

- **Set realistic goals.** They know there are twenty-four hours in a day, but they are guilty of what their parents often do— underestimating how long an activity will take and overscheduling their day.

- **Learn life principles.** Continue to teach them the principles that will govern their lives.

- **Try even if they are afraid.** Though teens want to accomplish great things, they doubt they have what it takes to make it happen. Fear of failure and criticism often causes teens to stand on the sidelines of life. Teach your child that failure is going to happen—but that through failure, their character is formed.

- **Embrace change.** Their world is changing quickly. Teach them the difference between embracing tools such as new technology and embracing moral decline. They must learn how to apply sound judgment.

- **Prepare for the unexpected.** Teens can become unraveled when life takes sudden, unexpected turns. Give them strategies that will help them cope with life situations.

- **Have space.** Space is necessary for growth and development. Not only do you need to respect their need to have time to think, but they also need to be taught the value of being alone. Teens have a lot on their minds, and having time to sort it all out is critical to their emotional well-being.

- **Develop a plan.** Some teens aren't good at planning. But knowing how to map out a plan helps them achieve their goals. When they learn to write down their ideas, they are able to visualize the pros and cons.

- **Be themselves.** Kids need to learn who they are and discover what is special about them. What talents do they possess that they can cultivate and use in the future?

- **Learn responsibility.** If they say they are going to do something, they should do it. Their words matter.

Teens want to discover truth, purpose, and meaning during this season of life. They want to be change agents, but all the options for doing so are overwhelming. Your teen needs you to help them sift through the possibilities and narrow down their focus. They know they can make a difference, but they may lack clarity on how they can do this. What they need are parents who will help them process and apply the information they are learning. They need your wisdom, not your facts. Teens don't follow us because we tell them to; they follow because they know we care about them. And most of all, they need us to be with them and for them as they navigate their increasing independence.

WRAPPING IT UP

- In what ways do you see your child changing?

- How can you help your child accept responsibility for their choices?

- What protection does your teen need?

- In what ways can you adjust your schedule to be more available to your teen?

Chapter 12

UNIQUELY CREATED

"Mom, I don't know what I'm good at or what I'm supposed to do when I grow up."

If I had a piece of chocolate for every time one of my kids made this statement, I would have enough delicious goodness to last a lifetime.

At some point (or at many points) in your teen's journey, the questions *Who am I?* and *What am I going to do with my life?* will come up. Some teens discover their interests, talents, and strengths without much anxiety, as my son Paul did. He is naturally good at math, logic, and problem-solving. All the personality quizzes and strengths tests pointed to engineering. He preferred a typical nine-to-five job with nights and weekends off. For Paul, knowing what he wanted to do wasn't a hard decision.

My daughter Jeannie, on the other hand, had a more difficult time. She is creative, artsy, and musically inclined. Though she received a full scholarship to the University of Central Florida like Paul, earning an A required more effort on her part. In any family, some things will come easily for one child while another child will struggle.

Throughout our children's teen years, my husband and I had multiple conversations with each of our children about IQ, strengths, personality, and the like. Helping your teen understand who they are requires a lot more than simply deciding to do so. And it goes much deeper than finding a direction for their life or settling on a career. Teens need to know their role or place in life. Teens are a wonder and a mystery. Knowing how they are wired is a step toward solving the puzzle.

If I asked you about yourself, you most likely would answer with what you do. *I'm a wife, I'm a stay-at-home mom, I'm a writer, I'm a nurse, I'm a teacher, I'm a doctor.* But those answers don't tell me who you are. Who you are and what you do are not the same thing. Who you are at your core is God's imprint on what is unique about you. At their core, peacemakers are peacemakers, achievers are achievers, talkers are talkers. The person God hardwired you to be doesn't change very much. Helping your teen understand how God has created them—and helping them see how that can inform what they do with their life—is not that complicated, but it does require intentionality and a few well-timed resources.

PERSONALITY VERSUS CHARACTER

Personality and character are two different things. Your character is shaped over time. Your environment, culture, friends, homelife, family values, and religious beliefs all play a part in developing character. Who has the greatest impact on your teen's character? Good news—it's you, the parents! If parents teach truth, honesty, respect, obedience, diligence, and perseverance throughout childhood, kids will grow up with these driving principles as their guide. The same is true if a parent abdicates his or her responsibility in this area and models dishonesty, disrespect, disobedience, carelessness, and laziness—a child will naturally acquire these undesirable qualities.

A child's personality, on other hand, is present from birth. From the time they're young, children give clues as to who they are and how they are designed. They may be bold or timid, focused or scattered, talkative or quiet. If your child is intuitive, sensitive, a thinker, an introvert, an extrovert, a feeler, or a perceiver, these are personality gifts God gave them as he formed them. Unless a traumatic event disrupts the growing-up process, these traits will not change much.

Intentional parents can learn a lot by what kids do and how they act. When parents understand personality, character, strengths, and temperament and teach their children in a loving, nurturing home, the dynamics within the family unit have the greatest opportunity for relational success. By knowing the quirks, thought processes, and temperament of your child, you will be able to meet them where they are so you can lead them where they need to go. When this happens, the child is properly prepared to transition into adulthood with less drama and fanfare.

What you are created to be or gifted to do often influences what you decide to do as a vocation. For example, my engineering son could do many things well. He became an advanced pianist, played a mean game of basketball, and could beat most of us at video games. His technical ability, learning style, and self-discipline helped him do well at those things. My creative daughter also became an advanced pianist, played basketball, and played her share of video games with her brothers. But her gifts for creating differed from those of her brother. Her gifts involved music, art, and photography. She intuitively knew how something should sound or look.

Both my son and my daughter are smart, diligent, hardworking, and creative. But the difference in their passions and talents led them to different vocations. Understanding that they are fearfully and wonderfully made—combined with knowing their unique gifts, strengths, and talents—minimized their need to compete against each other. The underlying acceptance of who they are also reduced the need to compare. Acquiring this knowledge and understanding took intentionality, time, and maturity for all of us.

When my kids were younger, I began to make conscious efforts to understand how they were wired. One way I did this was through watching what each of them liked to play with and how they used certain toys. Take Legos, for example. Did they open a new box of bricks and start assembling them without the directions, or did they look at the directions and sort out the pieces before they started to build the set? I paid attention to what they did, whether they were playing with new dolls or action figures or playing board games or learning something new. I made mental notes for a while before I realized I couldn't remember so many details. That's when I started a journal. I made a notebook for the family and placed dividers inside—one divider per family member. When I heard or saw them doing something that gave me a glimpse into who they are or what they enjoy doing, I wrote it in their section. I didn't write in it every day, but intentionally observing each child's unique approach to the world helped me gain a vision for who they were becoming.

Here are some examples of what this looked like:

- Likes to make gifts for siblings
- Shares their toys without being asked
- Enjoys reading for fun
- Constantly asks *Why?* questions
- Argues their point
- Has to be right
- Gets angry when they make a mistake
- Willing to give in to avoid conflict
- Tries to calm others down
- Gets so focused on what they are doing they lose track of time
- Blurts out their feelings without considering others

- Afraid to try new things alone
- Always makes others laugh
- Very detailed in what they do
- Gets frustrated when things don't go as planned
- Criticizes others
- Disappears when others are working
- Can't quit until the project is complete

Once a child reached middle school, I started to pay attention to which school subjects they enjoyed and which ones they complained about regularly. After a while, patterns began to emerge. I could see the makings of an engineer; the talents of an artist/musician; the eye of a videographer/script writer; the business skills of a budding young entrepreneur. That's when parenting teens started to get really exciting for me. I could start making recommendations based on things I knew they enjoyed. And on the flip side, I could help them see blind spots in their lives as well.

I don't know about you, but wouldn't you have loved to know what you were good at early in life? I sure would have. Most of us spend years trying to figure it out. We have the opportunity as parents to help our children understand their unique selves.

ASSESSMENTS

Believing we are all created *on* purpose *for* purpose is what draws me to various assessments. Many of us first encounter these kinds of assessments in the workplace, either during the interview process or during professional development. But why wait when we can start to identify these qualities in our children and help them understand how they are designed during the teen years?

Now, I offer a word of caution here. It's important to know how and when to introduce them to such details. When my youngest kids were in elementary school, I didn't try to explain information to them even though I knew it. They weren't mature enough yet to know what to do with it. And that is completely fine. You might not even want to use these resources until your child is older. I highly recommend that you discern what your child is ready for and when such information would be beneficial to them.

It's also important to note that no assessment is 100 percent accurate. No human-made test can tell a parent exactly how God has uniquely designed their child. Assessments are simply resources, tools designed to help us better understand ourselves and others.

The following are some of the assessments that my teens took or I helped them take:

- The 5 Love Languages
- CliftonStrengths / StrengthsQuest / StrengthsExplorer
- Myers-Briggs

Myers-Briggs, the 5 Love Languages, and CliftonStrengths aren't designed to put you or your teen in a box. They simply reveal the box you are already in. These are tools we can use to help build closer relationships while equipping our teens for adulthood.

The 5 Love Languages

Teens want to be loved, even teens who act as if they don't care. What many parents fail to realize is that how they themselves feel loved may not be how their children feel loved. Usually you and I show love to others the way we want to be shown love. When we understand how to love our teens in a way that connects deeply with them, our relationships can flourish.

In his book *The 5 Love Languages of Teenagers*, Dr. Gary Chapman explained what teenagers need and how to love them well. To do this, he went into great detail about the five ways people give and receive love:

- Words of affirmation
- Physical touch
- Quality time
- Acts of service
- Gifts

Chapman explained that there are "two periods in which parents often have heightened conflict with their children"—the so-called "terrible twos" and puberty.[1] These two seasons of childhood have one thing in common: the need for independence.

Every child will exert this desire at different times. It can come in the form of temper tantrums when he can't have his favorite toy or when she wants to hang out with friends and is told *no*. Some personalities will push for independence more than others. For example, my son Paul wanted peace and harmony, so his ways of seeking independence were subtle. He'd ask and remind us of his desire over and over and over. We thought he wanted to slowly wear us down. Jonathan, on the other hand, was willing to go head-to-head over everything. Even though conflict can't be avoided, we can address it in a healthy manner when we know how to love our kids.

Once I took the time to figure out how each of my children received love, I was able to be more intentional about what I did to strengthen our respective relationships. Knowing how to give love to my kids made parenting them easier. Observing what spoke love to each of them individually removed some of the guesswork. Some of my children need to hear gentle words, while others want me to stop what I'm doing and spend time with them. I stopped agonizing over buying them the perfect gift when folding their laundry was more effective. I stopped multitasking to play Go Fish with my quality-time daughter, Jaclyn.

I became more intentional about affirming Jeannie and Tyler instead of demanding that we need to spend time together.

Here are some specific ways you can speak each love language to your teen:

- **Words of affirmation:** Words of affirmation are life-giving to a teen with this primary love language. Negative, cruel comments or remarks have a greater impact on the heart of a teen whose primary love language is words of affirmation than on a teen with another primary love language. It's not that you can't correct someone who feels loved by words of affirmation; you just have to approach your conversations with extreme thought and care. I've had many teens tell me that all they hear from their parents is what they aren't doing right. I promise you, if you become intentional about affirming your teen first, they will be more open to changes you want them to make. Cutting put-downs don't roll off their back. Instead, they typically cause wounds, creating further barriers between you and your teen.

  So how do you parent a teen who needs words of affirmation? There are numerous ways to affirm your child, but I'll share three areas I've found the most helpful:

  - *Praise their accomplishments*: Be specific; general statements don't carry the same weight.
  - *Affirm who they are as a person in front of others*: Identify, praise, and celebrate their character traits.
  - *Speak words of affection*: "I love you"; "I enjoy your company"; "I feel proud to be your mom."

- **Physical touch:** Loving teens with the primary love language of physical touch might be a challenge for parents as their children mature. Showing love through touch (a hug, shoulder pat, holding hands) is a powerful way to create a strong connection. However, during the teen years, hugs, kisses, and pats on the back might not be as well received as they were when your child was younger. If you try to hug your teen in public, you're likely to experience some resistance, as he would rather wait until people aren't nearby. Teens often feel embarrassed in front of their peers, and having parents show affection exacerbates this. The key to loving a physical-touch teen is making sure it is an appropriate touch at an appropriate time and asking before initiating contact. Ask yourself the following questions to help you decide what and how much affection is appropriate:

- Is the physical touch for your teen, or are you the one needing a hug?
- Is it appropriate for the situation?
- Will they feel loved by your actions?

- **Quality time:** Showing love to the teen who needs quality time requires your undivided attention. They will not feel well loved if their parent is busy multitasking. They need togetherness. Time together needs to be intentional, and your teen needs to know it. To love your quality-time teen, turn off devices, be fully present, treat them as an adult, listen to their words, and watch their body language.

- **Acts of service:** Showing acts of service is not new to parents. We've been serving our children since their birth. But showing love to a child whose love language is acts of service requires deliberateness. My friend's dad washed her car and filled up the change holder with quarters, dimes, and nickels every Saturday. It meant so much to her. To teens, talk is cheap; they want action. The little things have meaning. Ask yourself these questions to love your teen in this way:

- Does this act speak to the heart of my teen?
- Is my reason to show love or to get something done?
- Is it the right time to do this for her?

- **Gifts:** Gift giving is the art of offering someone something they didn't earn or deserve—much like the gift of salvation. It can be a literal gift—like a necklace or a new outfit—or a date night to see their favorite movie or play. The key to gifts is that you shouldn't exchange gifts for behavior or use gifts as motivation. A genuine gift comes from the heart to express love—no strings attached.

  Before giving a gift, consider:

  - Will my teen be interested in the gift?
  - What is my motivation in giving the gift?
  - Will the gift be memorable?

Loving and being loved are the foundation of building close ties with your teen. Knowing about love languages is not enough. You have to implement this knowledge with your child. Learning to show love during this transformational season of life will greatly impact your future relationship. I encourage you to learn more about the love languages and use them to strengthen and grow your relationship with your teen.

Now that we have covered knowing our teens' love languages, let's turn our attention to discovering their strengths.

CliftonStrengths Assessment

In 2005, I attended an education workshop for parents and educators. During the training, I met Jenifer Fox, who later wrote *Your*

Child's Strengths[2] and who introduced me to strengths-based parenting and practical ways that parents and educators can teach kids using strengths. This approach piqued my interest right away. You see, most parents help their children improve weaknesses. For example, when a child gets five As and one C, we ask her why she didn't get all As. But in strengths-based parenting, the parent teaches to the child's strengths—noting where the child excels and helping them lean into those areas. As Fox pointed out, "Contrary to popular belief, the opposite of strength is not weakness. The opposite of strength is depletion. If an activity is not engaging an individual's strengths, thereby energizing the person, the activity is depleting."[3] By focusing on weaknesses, we ignore the gift of strengths that our children possess. We don't ignore our teens' weaknesses; we teach them how to manage them.

The main resource for strengths-based learning is *StrengthsFinder 2.0* by Tom Rath, which is based on the work of Donald O. Clifton. You can access the accompanying assessment online to discern your strengths.[4]

While the CliftonStrengths assessment might be too advanced for some teens, Clifton Youth StrengthsExplorer is designed for children ages ten to fourteen years old. Gallup research was used to create this assessment, which focuses on helping youth discover and develop the unique talents within them. Of course, truly understanding strengths and weaknesses takes time. But this assessment can be a helpful springboard for your family.

Myers-Briggs Type Indicator

Of all the assessments, the Myers-Briggs Type Indicator (MBTI), a personality assessment, is the one my daughters and I discuss the most. Myers-Briggs serves as a tool to discover more about your personality and how that translates into a vocation and affects your relationships.[5] It's an easy assessment for teens to understand, and it's fun to explore together.

I use this assessment to understand why my kids do what they do and say what they say. When I understand where my kids are coming from, I'm able to teach and communicate with them more effectively. And as my kids learn about me and each other through this assessment, they become more patient with one another's differences.

Understanding personality types allows you to see through another person's lens, reducing the friction between two points of view. Instead of labeling a person as *bad* or *good* based on behavior, parents can adjust their approach, treating their teens with more empathy.

THE QUEST

When we learn to use the lenses our teens look through, we truly accept them for who they are—allowing them the ability to grow into the real people God created them to be. There is value in respecting the unique human God gave you to raise for his glory.

Teens have little say in their circumstances or surroundings. When we think about their lives through their eyes, we can gain new perspective that will help us appreciate every part of who they are.

As you seek to parent your unique teen, lovingly remember these things:

- They didn't choose their parents.
- They didn't choose their school.
- They didn't choose their zip code.
- They didn't choose their birth order.
- They didn't choose their siblings.
- They didn't choose whether they were planned or not.
- They didn't make the rules.
- They didn't choose.

Once you start to understand your teen and how they're uniquely crafted, you're less likely to get upset when your commanding child wants to control you. You learn to recognize their strength of determination as a gift in need of tempering. Though they will sometimes need correction, your reaction to their commanding temperament will be designed according to what works with that child. Their approach may need correcting, but that strength of will is part of how God created your child. Or when your compliant child struggles to make a decision, you'll be careful not to shame or embarrass them for that inability. They need to be understood and guided.

Tyler, my middle child, had a hard time making decisions when he was growing up. His peacemaking, adaptable personality meant he was happy to go with the flow. He was never really pushed to make many decisions because he always had options. At any given time, he could bounce back and forth between the big kids and the little kids. It's not that he didn't want to decide; he was just incredibly thoughtful and kind. He always wanted to consider others first. That's a mother's dream child, right?

As he entered college, Tyler had a harder time. He could no longer follow others. It was time for him to decide his own future. We watched and listened to how he went about this process. I'll be honest; there were times we got frustrated because it was so hard for him. We just wanted to say, "Come on, it's not that difficult. Do you want tacos or pizza? Vanilla or chocolate? Do you want to watch *Lord of the Rings* or *Star Wars*?" But the truth is, it was hard for him. He was formed and fashioned to be who he is. He eventually learned to work it out, but it took until he was in his twenties. The truth is, he will never be the type of man to make rash or quick decisions. We love and respect that trait in him, and so does his beautiful wife.

Your teen will step, stumble, and bump into who they are little by little. Be gentle with them. Use your adult reasoning skills to offer insights from what you've read, and draw from the things you already know. Don't belittle them because they can't decide which pair of shoes to wear or whether they really want to try out for soccer. Instead, guide them and help them make decisions until they're ready to make them on their own. They're in the process of becoming an adult. Every day, your teen learns more about life and how to navigate the unexpected twists and turns associated with it. Check your expectations of where you think they should be—stop thinking they are behind or ahead. They are simply at a point along their journey, and you get to help them move to the next point. I implore you to pay attention and not ignore what you notice. Then carefully speak into their tender heart through your soft whispers and late-night text conversations.

Teens are on a quest to discover more about who they are and where they fit in. As they mature, the desire to know their purpose intensifies. This is why time invested in studying and understanding the unique personality and strengths of your teen will help you be a better parent and enjoy a stronger bond with your child.

WRAPPING IT UP

- What are the potential benefits of your teen's learning how to excel at their strengths and manage their weaknesses in a positive way?

- In what ways has learning about your teen's strengths and love languages helped you be a better parent?

- Are you battling a strong, commanding child? Or trying to encourage a submissive, compliant child? List three steps you can take to help that child be the person they are designed to be.

- What questions could you ask your commanding or compliant child to help them fully understand how God made them?

CELEBRATE
THE TEEN YEARS

Have you ever ordered a "pour over" at a coffee shop? The barista grinds the coffee beans and puts them in the top of the coffeepot, and then takes hot water and pours it over the coffee. It's a slow process; the water drips one little drop at a time. But waiting produces a very flavorful cup of coffee.

This is where your teen is. As they grew up, you provided everything they needed to become a productive adult and fulfill their calling. Now, in the teen years, you're adding the hot water of trust and independence. It filters one drop at a time—they make a decision, and then another, and another . . . until you have a picture of this amazing person who will do great things for the Lord and who you get to enjoy life with. And that is something to celebrate!

The notion of celebrating the teen years may seem like an oxymoron. I'm not saying it's easy, but I can promise you this: You absolutely can celebrate this season of life with your kid—even when things get hard or go wrong or conflicts arise.

Do you remember when your child was a toddler trying to do something for the first time and they refused help, declaring, "I do it!"? You lovingly watched them struggle and try until they finally figured it out. You were so excited and you cheered them on. Then, by the time your child was seven or eight years old, they were grasping larger concepts, and you celebrated as they practiced real acts of kindness toward you or their siblings.

You've spent so much time pouring into your kid, teaching them life skills—from how to ride a bike to how to cook, clean, brush their teeth, and get dressed. Now you can watch them put it all together. They get to start making real-life decisions on their own. (Or at least they think they're on their own!) You want them to have that confidence throughout their teen years.

The milestones in their life are even bigger—steps toward independence and greater responsibility. Driving, relationships, school decisions. You have to trust in what you've invested in them up to this point. They will start taking all the things you have taught them, all the stuff that is in their brain, and filtering it into their heart. Just as when they were little, these steps deserve celebration.

LIFE IS A RIVER

Picture your family on a small inflatable boat, the kind used for whitewater rafting. The guide pushes the boat into the river, and everyone settles in their place, paddling and enjoying the calm water. As you travel downstream, the river starts to get a little bumpy. You hit a few rocks, but all is well. Then the water becomes increasingly difficult to navigate. People are yelling at each other to hold on, to paddle harder. Some are excited by the ride, while others fear what lies ahead. No one can see beyond the bend. Will things be smooth as they were when you started, or will they get worse? Smiles fade and tensions rise as you face the roughest part of the river. Suddenly the boat dips, and your son falls out. Panic sets in. You paddle harder than you thought possible to reach him before he drowns. Navigating the water isn't as fun as when you began.

That's the nature of parenting teens and part of why it's exciting and worth celebrating. You don't know what's around the corner, and every day seems to bring a new crisis or a new exciting event in your teen's life. Determine to enjoy this! Every twist and turn is shaping your teen's life. Help them understand that the defeat at the basketball game or the grade on the test they studied so hard for is genuinely okay because it's only a moment in time. The event does not define them—the lessons they learn, the preparations for the future, are what make them who they will become. Teach your teen to work through the bumps, pitfalls, and whitewater situations of life, and let them know they will not be consumed. Though they get knocked down, they can get back up. The future is something to anticipate with excitement; neither you nor your teen needs to fear what's ahead.

God did not give us teenagers as a curse; this time with our kids is not meant to be negative. We can cement trust, listen intently, and point them to Christ. We may face conflict and difficulties, but we can't let those experiences overwhelm our perception of this season. We have so many things to celebrate.

The teenage years are the big send-off. Every day pushes your child closer toward adulthood, when they will accept responsibility for every action and take their place in society. One day, you may get to enjoy their wedding, and maybe even be a grandparent. One day, they may help you through a health crisis or act as your caregiver at the end of your life. Whatever career your child has, whatever they do and wherever they go, you are creating a legacy. That legacy goes way beyond the teen years: It will impact your child's children and their children's children.

That's what you get to help shape, and that's what you get the opportunity to embrace. That's your family story. Our kids read us—in fact, they're afraid when we're afraid, they're excited when we're excited, and they grieve when we grieve. If your teen hurts, the family hurts, and if they rejoice, the family rejoices. They need to know that this is their family and that you will tackle the world together.

If you have multiple children, the reality is that one will be more popular than another, or smarter academically than another, or have more musical ability than another. You need to embrace every bit of who your children are as individuals—both their strengths and their weaknesses. Teach them to embrace their siblings' strengths and weaknesses too. Teach them to celebrate and be glad for another sibling's accomplishments and grieve for another sibling's sorrow.

As you intentionally cultivate a community of support and celebration, you will create an environment that's so attractive, so sweet and inviting, that your child won't want to miss it. The sense of belonging they'll experience will makes them think twice about everything they do because they don't want to live in a world that's all about them. They'll want to belong in a world that involves their family.

If you have done everything "right" but the masterpiece looks more like an abstract than a Monet, don't stop painting. Keep adding new colors to your painter's palette; God is not finished. Recommit your child to him, and ask him to help you see blind spots in your parenting. Even if the paint dries, it can always be changed. You always have the opportunity to add new coats of forgiveness, wisdom, and maturity.

LIFE ABUNDANT

Think back to that slow-drip coffee. You eagerly await that cup of coffee you carefully brewed. But you've got to wait for the finished product. And sometimes you may not like the process—before it's finished, the coffee may be too strong or too weak or in a flavor you weren't expecting. But as you parent your teen, remember that you're working with the end in mind. Soon, you'll be launching your teen out into the world, but you have been walking through these years with a vision of enjoying life together. If you invest in the relationship, if you keep your child's heart well, you'll still be connected when they reach adulthood. You will still have this closeness of heart and sweetness of relationship.

God gave us life to live and live abundantly. As your teen progresses in years, you progress from telling to teaching to training to coaching to cheerleading. When your kid starts to make their own decisions, you get to be the one who celebrates with them and cheers for them, and you can be the one they come to when they're hurt. You get to pray for them, laugh with them, and cry with them, but the important thing is that you're the one who gets to experience life with them. Keep loving them.

You can have more freedom in your parenting. Parent with principles, not from rules. When you focus less on rules and embrace principles in the teen years, you learn to trust God with your teen in a much deeper way. You can have more confidence and joy, knowing that you're pursuing a larger vision. Parenting your teen is not just about today or tomorrow; you're striving for something bigger: for your child to walk in all truth.

And if you're discouraged because strife and resentment have entered your home, God reminds us that it's never too late. He is the God of redemption and hope. The river may twist and turn, but God sees the whole thing. He knows where the river begins and where it rushes into the ocean. He has everything under control and has a plan for you and your family. As you strive to help your child understand the plan God has for their life, doing the best you can with your human limitations and imperfections, he works in you and through you.

Teenagers often get a bad rap. Society often stereotypes them in negative ways. But they are simply young people yearning to grow up. They ask tough questions about what they see taking place around them. May we be the ones they ask for clarity and truth!

You are in a battle for the heart and soul of your child. The way to win is by parenting beyond the rules. Cultivate a relationship of trust, not fear. Don't let others win the battle and influence your teen. God has chosen you to parent your teen. You are the primary creator of their memories; make good ones.

Make no mistake: God never said it would be easy or that raising a teen into adulthood would be effortless. But, dear parent, the assignment you've been given is one to be embraced and celebrated. Your family is so much more than a collection of people who share the same last name and living room. To build the family God desires, you must be alert and involved. Your relentless pursuit of authentic relationships will be rewarded. Take every opportunity to teach your child in the way they should go. God has great plans for your family.

Don't be fooled into thinking your kid doesn't need you. They rely on your steadfast love to help them navigate the world they live in. As you intentionally speak loving words at the right time or ask a question at the appropriate moment, you help build a relationship with your child that will last well beyond the current season of parenting. They'll know that you have their best interests in mind, even when they don't appreciate it.

As you model the importance of family first, your teen is learning the real meaning of having such a strong support system. You can walk together as a family. You can enjoy the small relational victories. You can look forward to the exciting years ahead. And you can and will celebrate the teen years.

When your teen emerges into adulthood, you will get to experience a joy that is the answer to countless prayers and hundreds of late-night conversations.

Never stop painting pictures of possibilities for your family. I pray your adult child will one day look back on their childhood and say, "Thank you, Mom and Dad, for never giving up on me. Thank you for teaching me the truth of who God is and who I am in him. Thank you for helping me get through some hard times. Thank you for being faithful."

WRAPPING IT UP

* What are you doing right now to celebrate the teen years?

* How will focusing on celebrating the teen years change your outlook on parenting teens?

* Reflect on three specific areas in your relationship with your teen that you can intentionally celebrate.

RESOURCES
TO GO DEEPER

- *Understanding Your Teen: Shaping Their Character, Facing Their Realities* by Jim Burns
- *It's Not Too Late: The Essential Part You Play in Shaping Your Teen's Faith* by Dan Dupee
- *Screens and Teens: Connecting with Our Kids in a Wireless World* by Kathy Koch
- *The Tech-Wise Family: Everyday Steps for Putting Technology in Its Proper Place* by Andy Crouch
- *Right Click: Parenting Your Teenager in a Digital Media World* by Art Bamford, Kara Powell, and Brad M. Griffin
- *Love Does: Discover a Secretly Incredible Life in an Ordinary World* by Bob Goff
- *The Lifegiving Table: Nurturing Faith through Feasting, One Meal at a Time* by Sally Clarkson
- *The 5 Love Languages of Teenagers: The Secret to Loving Teens Effectively* by Gary Chapman
- *When God Writes Your Love Story* by Eric Ludy and Leslie Ludy
- *Passion and Purity: Learning to Bring Your Love Life under Christ's Control* by Elisabeth Elliot

- *Every Young Woman's Battle: Guarding Your Mind, Heart, and Body in a Sex-Saturated World* by Shannon Ethridge and Stephen Arterburn
- *Boundaries: When to Say Yes, How to Say No to Take Control of Your Life* by Henry Cloud and John Townsend
- *Wild at Heart: Discovering the Secret of a Man's Soul* by John Eldredge
- *Preparing Your Son for Every Man's Battle: Honest Conversations about Sexual Integrity* by Stephen Arterburn, Fred Stoeker, and Mike Yorkey

ACKNOWLEDGMENTS

Writing this book has been the fulfillment of God's whisper many years ago. It took a small army of people, too. God used several people to teach and influence me and to shape my views on parenting. They showed me how to build relationships by their example. I watched how they parented their teens. I asked questions and listened intently to what they shared, tucking away those wise words deep in my heart. I'm indebted to each mentor who took me under their wing and taught an inexperienced mother how to build a close family. The first thing I learned is to never give up on your teen. Though my children didn't always make wise decisions, they needed me to remain steadfast and devoted to them. Second, I learned that unconditional love given to my children became the bridge to restore right relationships within the family. And third, I learned that it was possible to enjoy this season of parenting if I looked for things to celebrate.

Much appreciation for my faithful prayer warriors. You believed in this project from day one. Your prayers kept me going, even when I doubted myself. My dearest friends, you know who you are. You have watched me walk through the parenting journey. You know the struggles I've faced along the way, yet you continue to love my family and me. I love you and your precious families. I've loved doing life together, and I'm so grateful to you.

To my writer friends, Erin, Kristin, Katie, Vanessa, Michelle: Your encouragement got me through the book-writing process. I love how you've modeled women helping other women for the sake of Christ. It's been an honor to share this experience with you.

Much love and thanks to my dear friend Jackie Kilpatrick for tirelessly using your editing skills to help make this book possible. You pulled too many late nights listening, editing, and fleshing out the words that fill these pages. Words cannot express how thankful I am for our friendship. Such a gift. Our time spent together was a treasure for which I'm forever grateful to you.

Heather Paquette, thank you for saying *yes* when you didn't even know me. You poured countless hours into helping me decide what to write. Our Panera dates became the highlight of my week. I treasure your friendship and admire your writing savvy. You are a puzzle-piece master.

Special thanks to Blythe McIntosh Daniel, my agent and my friend. You've walked with me through some tough times. Your encouragement kept me moving forward. Thank you!

To David Zimmerman, Don Pape, Caitlyn Carlson, Elizabeth Schroll, Olivia Eldredge, Melissa Myers, Robin Bermel, and the rest of the NavPress and Tyndale House team: Your prayers and support for this book were unmatched. I'm honored to work with such an outstanding group of professionals. Caitlyn, you were an answer to many prayers. Thank you for pulling out the best and cutting the rest.

To all the Equipped to Be moms: This book is for you. All your emails, conversations, texts, and meet-ups encouraged me to press on even when Mom was ill. May your families grow stronger in this season of parenting. It's my prayer that the relationships between you and your teens will last beyond the teen years.

I close with the way I began. Paul, Jeannie, Tyler, Jaclyn, and Jonathan: You are the reason behind this book. You cheered me on when I got weary. You took me to lunch and Walt Disney World when I needed a break. You forgave me countless times when I stumbled as a mom. Every word in this book is because of you. I love you without condition. Thank you for loving me and teaching me the joy of being a mom.

My deepest gratitude goes to Tom. What can I say? Thank you for your unwavering support of the high calling of motherhood. You prayed for me, wrote beautiful notes, sent "I love you" flowers, and constantly encouraged me to embrace motherhood. Thank you for letting our home be the teen hangout. We have made hundreds of memories with all those kids. I love you, now and forever!

ABOUT THE AUTHOR

CONNIE ALBERS is a speaker, mother of five young adults, and writer who strengthens families and leaders. She has been a spokesperson for a Fortune 500 company, director and board member for a non-profit state homeschool organization, senior strategist for a successful US congressional campaign, and director of first impressions for Social Media Marketing World. You can follow Connie at www .conniealbers.com and https://www.facebook.com/ConnieAlbers .Author. For more information about *Parenting beyond the Rules*, go to parentingbeyondtherules.com.

NOTES

CHAPTER 1: WHEN THE DREAM CHANGES

1. Kendra Cherry, "Authoritative Parenting: Characteristics and Effects," Verywell Mind, October 5, 2018, https://www.verywellmind.com/what -is-authoritative-parenting-2794956.

2. Anna Almendrala, "5 Signs You Were Raised by Helicopter Parents," *HuffPost,* September 30, 2015, https://www.huffingtonpost.com/entry/5-ways-to-tell -you-were-raised-by-helicopter-parents_us_5609de6ee4b0dd850308e260.

3. Karen Fancher, "The Rise of the Lawnmower Parent," *Pittsburgh Moms Blog,* June 25, 2016, https://pittsburgh.citymomsblog.com/mom/rise -lawnmower-parent/.

4. WeAreTeachers Staff, "Lawnmower Parents Are the New Helicopter Parents and We Are Not Here for It," We Are Teachers, August 30, 2018, https://www .weareteachers.com/lawnmower-parents/.

CHAPTER 2: THE FOUNDATION OF RELATIONSHIPS

1. Richard Plass and James Cofield, *The Relational Soul: Moving from False Self to Deep Connection* (Downers Grove, IL: InterVarsity Press, 2014), 12.

2. Plass and Cofield, *Relational Soul,* 12.

3. Plass and Cofield, *Relational Soul,* 12.

4. Charles Feltman, *The Thin Book of Trust: An Essential Primer for Building Trust at Work* (Bend, OR: Thin Book Publishing, 2009), 13–14.

5. Feltman, *Trust,* 14.

CHAPTER 3: EQUIPPED TO LOVE

1. See chapter 12 for more on love languages and strengths.

CHAPTER 5: PAINTING POSSIBILITIES

1. Amy Ellis Nutt, "Why Kids and Teens May Face Far More Anxiety These Days," *Washington Post*, May 10, 2018, https://www.washingtonpost.com /news/to-your-health/wp/2018/05/10/why-kids-and-teens-may-face-far -more-anxiety-these-days/?noredirect=on&utm_term=.9e40df081bac.

CHAPTER 6: UNDERSTAND THEIR WORLD

1. *Merriam-Webster*, s.v. "observe," accessed September 4, 2018, https://www .merriam-webster.com/dictionary/observe.
2. Kathy Koch, *Screens and Teens: Connecting with Our Kids in a Wireless World* (Chicago: Moody, 2015).
3. Jim Burns, *Understanding Your Teen: Shaping Their Character, Facing Their Realities* (Downers Grove, IL: InterVarsity, 2017), 62.
4. Burns, *Understanding Your Teen*, 141.
5. Guyana Inc. Staff, "Bullying and Suicide: What Is Bullying?" *Guyana Inc.*, accessed September 4, 2018, http://guyanainc.biz/columns/bullying-suicide -what-is-bullying/.

CHAPTER 8: MONITOR YOUR MOUTH

1. Exception: Walking out of the room is advisable when a heated exchange threatens to lead to hurtful words. See page 132.

CHAPTER 9: TACKLE TOUGH TOPICS

1. For example, see Mark 10:6-9; Hebrews 13:4; Leviticus 18:22; Romans 1:26-28; 1 Corinthians 6:9-11, 17-20; Jude 1:5-8; and 1 Timothy 1:8-11.
2. "Addiction by the Numbers," Center on Addiction, accessed September 18, 2018, https://www.centeronaddiction.org/.
3. René A. Arrazola, Shanta R. Dube, and Brian A. King, "Tobacco Product Use among Middle and High School Students—United States, 2011 and 2012," *Morbidity and Mortality Weekly Report* 62, no. 45 (November 15, 2013): 893–97. Also see René A. Arrazola et al., "Tobacco Use among Middle and High School Students—United States, 2013," *Morbidity and Mortality Weekly Report* 63, no. 45 (November 14, 2014): 1021–26.
4. "About E-Cigarettes," Center on Addiction, accessed September 6, 2018, https://www.centeronaddiction.org/e-cigarettes/about-e-cigarettes.
5. "Youth and Tobacco Use," Centers for Disease Control and Prevention, accessed September 6, 2018, https://www.cdc.gov/tobacco/data_statistics /fact_sheets/youth_data/tobacco_use/index.htm.
6. Linda Richter, "E-Cigarettes: Weighing the Pros and Cons," Center on Addiction, September 2018, https://www.centeronaddiction.org/e-cigarettes /about-e-cigarettes/e-cigarettes-weighing-pros-and-cons.

7. Emily Feinstein, "E-Cigarettes 101: What Parents Should Know about E-Cigarettes," September 2018, https://www.centeronaddiction.org/e-cigarettes/about-e-cigarettes/what-parents-should-know-about-e-cigarettes.
8. Feinstein, "E-Cigarettes 101."
9. The Bible is full of encouraging words for anxious or fearful hearts. I encourage you to find pertinent verses that will speak to your child's heart during a difficult time and share them with your teen.
10. Here are a few Scripture references to get you started: Deuteronomy 31:6, Joshua 1:5, and 1 Chronicles 28:20 (I like how the New King James Bible words these verses).
11. The Bible offers many reminders that God is in control and we have no need to fear. See, for example, Psalm 46:10, Isaiah 41:10, Matthew 6:25-34, John 16:33, and Philippians 4:6-7.

CHAPTER 10: SQUASH YOUR FEAR

1. Max Lucado includes a similar line in one of his books: "Feed your fears, and your faith will starve. Feed your faith, and your fears will." Max Lucado, *Fearless: Imagine Your Life without Fear* (Nashville, TN: Thomas Nelson, 2009), 74.
2. For example, see Deuteronomy 11:19, Proverbs 29:17, and 1 Timothy 5:8.

CHAPTER 12: UNIQUELY CREATED

1. Gary Chapman, *The 5 Love Languages of Teenagers: The Secret to Loving Teens Effectively* (Chicago: Northfield, 2016), 226.
2. Jenifer Fox, *Your Child's Strengths: Discover Them, Develop Them, Use Them* (New York: Viking, 2008).
3. Fox, *Your Child's Strengths*, 172.
4. The assessment isn't free, but I've found that the benefits of knowing your top five strengths (or, if you prefer, how you rank in all thirty-four strength categories) outweigh the cost. See https://www.gallupstrengthscenter.com/store/en-us/assessments.
5. "Personality and Careers," The Myers & Briggs Foundation, accessed September 7, 2018, https://www.myersbriggs.org/type-use-for-everyday-life/personality-and-careers/; "Psychological Type and Relationships," The Myers & Briggs Foundation, accessed September 7, 2018, http://www.myersbriggs.org/type-use-for-everyday-life/psychological-type-and-relationships/.